MISBEHAVIOR · RidiCule
...on · UnPopulaR · Edgier
inSPIRATION · FAST
im · IMAGINATION · BURST · LOUD
tion · EXPLoDe Queer
ysterious · Flexible
MAD · Passionate · BITING
disorder · overkill · overkill ·
· Textural · IMPACT ·
· AGGressive · PunCh
· Graffitti · PunK !
ze · Collage · Gutty ·
gerous · UNLIMITED · Vision

The Collector's Series
Unique Marketing Resource Books From PBC

■ **CLIO AWARDS**
  by the CLIO Organization
  A tribute to 30 years of advertising excellence. 496 pages.
  9" x 12" hardbound with jacket. Over 500 full-color illustrations.
  $75.00

■ **CLIO AWARDS — PART 1**
  by the CLIO Organization
  An historical volume on the world of advertising. 280 pages.
  9" x 12" paperbound. Over 250 full-color illustrations.
  $45.00

■ **CLIO AWARDS — PART 2**
  by the CLIO Organization
  The authoritative guide to the 30th annual CLIO competition.
  192 pages. 9" x 12" paperbound. Over 100 full-color illustrations.
  $40.00

■ **INTERNATIONAL ADVERTISING DESIGN**
  edited by Philip Kleinman
  A global array of successful print advertising campaigns. 192 pages.
  8 1/2" x 11" hardbound with jacket. Over 300 full-color illustrations.
  $55.00

■ **INTERNATIONAL ADVERTISING DESIGN 2**
  edited by Philip Kleinman
  The second sourcebook in the series of leading worldwide print campaigns. 192 pages. 8 1/2" x 11" hardbound with jacket.
  Over 400 full-color illustrations.
  $55.00

■ **THE BEST OF RETAIL ADVERTISING**
  *by the National Retail Merchants Association
  (National Retail Federation)*
  Award-winning retail advertising graphics. 256 pages.
  9" x 12" hardbound with jacket. Over 200 full-color illustrations.
  $60.00

Order Now!
Toll Free	In NY State	FAX
800-527-2826	516-676-2727	516-676-2738

QTY.	TITLE	PRICE	TOTAL ($)

Order Total $_____
Shipping / Handling (USA-10%, outside USA-15% of Order Total) $_____
Sub-Total $_____
NY State Residents Add Local Sales Tax $_____
ORDER TOTAL $_____

Name_____ Phone_____
Company_____ Title_____
Address_____
City/St. Zip_____ Country_____

METHOD OF PAYMENT
____ Money Orders Payable to **PBC International, Inc.**
____ MasterCard ____ Visa ____ Am Ex
Card #_____ Expiration Date_____
Signature_____

Send completed order coupon with payment to:
PBC INTERNATIONAL, INC., One School Street, Glen Cove, NY 11542, USA
PLEASE ALLOW 10-12 WEEKS FOR DELIVERY

COLL

CREATIVITY...*starts here!*

Inspirational Books from PBC

■ **SALES PROMOTION DESIGN**
by Robert B. Konikow
Innovative and result-producing campaigns. 256 pages.
9" x 12" hardbound with jacket. Over 300 full-color illustrations.
$60.00

■ **DIRECT MARKETING DESIGN 2**
by Richard Harbert and the Direct Marketing Creative Guild
Creativity in direct response advertising. 256 pages.
9" x 12" hardbound with jacket. Over 300 full-color illustrations.
$60.00

■ **POINT OF PURCHASE DESIGN 2**
by Robert B. Konikow
An extensive compilation of attractive and cost-effective POP displays. 256 pages. 9" x 12" hardbound with jacket. Over 300 full-color illustrations.
$60.00

■ **PACKAGING DESIGN 4**
by Charles Biondo and the Packaging Design Council International
An inspiring array of leading global package designs. 256 pages.
9" x 12" hardbound with jacket. Over 350 full-color illustrations.
$60.00

■ **DESIGNERS' SELF-IMAGE**
by Joshua Marcus based on an Israel Museum Exhibition
International identity graphics and programs. 224 pages.
9" x 12" hardbound with jacket. Over 250 full-color illustrations.
$55.00

■ **INTERNATIONAL VIDEO GRAPHIC DESIGN**
by Jack M. Beebe
A global spotlight on today's video graphics. 192 pages.
9" x 12" hardbound with jacket. Over 250 full-color illustrations.
$55.00

■ **GRAPHIC EXCELLENCE**
by the editors of Studio Magazine
The artistry of leading graphic designs. 192 pages.
9" x 12" paperbound. Over 250 full-color illustrations.
$35.00

FREE when you order two or more books!

Order Now!

Toll Free	In NY State	FAX
800-527-2826	516-676-2727	516-676-2738

QTY. TITLE PRICE TOTAL ($)

Order Total $_____
Shipping / Handling (USA-10%, outside USA-15% of Order Total) $_____
Sub-Total $_____
NY State Residents Add Local Sales Tax $_____
ORDER TOTAL $_____

Name_____ Phone_____
Company_____ Title_____
Address_____
City/St. Zip_____ Country_____

METHOD OF PAYMENT
____ Money Orders Payable to **PBC International, Inc.**
____ MasterCard ____ Visa ____ Am Ex
Card #_____ Expiration Date_____
Signature_____

Send completed order coupon with payment to:
PBC INTERNATIONAL, INC., One School Street, Glen Cove, NY 11542, USA
PLEASE ALLOW 10-12 WEEKS FOR DELIVERY

CRE

NON
TRADITIONAL
DESIGN

Innovative Approaches to Graphics

NON TRADITIONAL DESIGN

MIKE QUON

Library of Applied Design

An Imprint of

PBC INTERNATIONAL, INC.

Distributor to the book trade in the United States and Canada:
Rizzoli International Publications Inc.
300 Park Avenue South
New York, NY 10010

Distributor to the art trade in the United States and Canada:
PBC International, Inc.
One School Street
Glen Cove, NY 11542
1-800-527-2826
Fax 516-676-2738

Distributor throughout the rest of the world:
Hearst Books International
1350 Avenue of the Americas
New York, NY 10019

Copyright © 1992 by
PBC INTERNATIONAL, Inc.
All rights reserved. No part of this book may be reproduced in any
form whatsoever without written permission of the copyright owner,
PBC INTERNATIONAL, INC.
One School Street, Glen Cove, NY 11542.

Library of Congress Cataloging-in-Publication Data

Quon, Mike.
    Non-traditional design / by Mike Quon.
       p.   cm.
    Includes index.
    ISBN 0-86636-179-0
    1. Design--History--20th century--Themes, motives.   I. Title.
NK1390.Q66   1992
745.4'442--dc20   91-45757
                                                                                     CIP

CAVEAT—Information in this text is believed accurate, and will pose no problem for the
student or casual reader. However, the author was often constrained by information contained
in signed release forms, information that could have been in error or not included at all. Any
misinformation (or lack of information) is the result of failure in these attestations. The author
has done whatever is possible to insure accuracy.

Color separation, printing and binding by
Toppan Printing Co. (H.K.) Ltd. Hong Kong

Typography by
TypeLink, Inc.

Printed in Hong Kong

10 9 8 7 6 5 4 3 2 1

"I would prefer to invent a grammar of my own than to bind myself to rules which do not belong to me."
Henry David Thoreau

"Any Fool Can Make a Rule."
Pablo Picasso

TABLE OF

Introduction	**8**
Alexander Isley	**18**
Nippon Design Center	**20**
Concrete	**24**
Douglas Design Office	**26**
Allen Hori	**28**
Jesse Reyes	**32**
Weller Institute for the Cure of Design	**34**
Hot House	**36**
Granary Books	**38**
OLIO	**40**
Spider Webb	**41**
Paul Davis	**42**
Corey Edmonds Millen	**46**
Wing Chan	**48**
Ink Tank	**50**
Thirst	**52**
Lloyd Ziff	**56**
Worksight	**58**
Paper Moon Graphics	**60**
AGI	**62**

CONTENTS

Waters Design Associates Inc.	64	Stylism	120
Makoto Saito	66	Javier Romero	122
Chris Harvey	72	Shin Matsunaga Design	124
Siebert Design	74	Eskind Waddell	128
Frans Lieshout	76	Studio Seireeni	130
Chip Kidd	78	plus design, inc.	134
Mike Salisbury	80	Partners Design Group	136
Edwin Torres	84	Sibley/Peteet	138
Mike Quon	86	Rico Lins	140
Michael Peters Ltd.	90	BJ Krivanek	144
Art Chantry	92	MTV Creative Services	146
Milton Glaser	94	Metropolis	150
Army Trainer Magazine	96	Gary Panter	152
Blackdog Design	98	Alan Chan	156
Cranbrook Academy of Art	100	Jacobs Fulton Design	158
M & Co.	102	David Carson Design	160
2029	104	Maria Grillo	164
Anthony Ma	106	Creative Black Book	166
Faith	110	Emigre Graphics	170
Harry Metzler	116	Russo Sicard Studio	172
Earl Gee	118		
Fred/Alan Inc.	119		

Appendix **174**

References and Suggested Reading **175**

Acknowledgments **176**

Index **177**

notes

When I was approached about selecting

"THE PRESENT IS FILLED WITH FLOTSAM AND JETSAM

material for this book, two questions came

AND IRONY AND CHAOS AND DISORDER IN ALL ARENAS,

immediately to mind: What is non traditional

POLITICAL AND SOCIOLOGICAL. AND THIS IS REFLECTED

design? On the flip side, what is traditional

IN EVERY FORM OF THE ARTS. I THINK WE HAVE TO

design? And, how are the two related?

WORK IN THE PRESENT EVEN IF IT'S NOT NECESSARILY

GOOD, EVEN IF WE DON'T UNDERSTAND IT OURSELVES.

Barely a generation ago, graphic design and

YOU ONLY FIND OUT 10, MAYBE 20 YEARS LATER, WHAT

advertising were called "commercial art"

WAS GOING ON."

and were fairly simple in their ideas and

Frank Gehry

EXECUTION. THEY CONTAINED EASY TO READ AND UNDERSTAND MESSAGES. FRANKLIN GOTHIC, GARAMOND OR HELVETICA WERE THE TYPEFACES OF CHOICE. A TEAPOT WAS EASILY RECOGNIZABLE AS A TEAPOT, EVEN AT A DISTANCE.

> "Art Is What You Can Get Away With."
> — Andy Warhol

CHANGE IS ALL AROUND US, HOWEVER, AND ITS RATE HAS BEEN TREMENDOUSLY ACCELERATED BY THE PACE OF THE ELECTRONIC AGE AND THE SPEED, VERSATILITY and flexibility of computers, television and fax machines. Styles change in a matter of months, weeks, days or even minutes—not years. Increasingly, designers are blurring the traditionally defined boundaries of their profession. Today we see graphic designers crossing over into three

dimensional design, and industrial designers getting involved in graphics and

interiors. There is no longer any one way to design, no single set of standards or

rules, no "ideal" design style.

"Less is more."

Ludwig Mies van der Rohe

Throughout my career, I've noticed a lot of eye-catching work that doesn't fit into

the categories of so-called traditional design. For example, art and design inspired

by the alternately exuberant and sinister energy of street art, urban graffiti, and the

underground movement all fall outside the parameters of what was once considered

tasteful, appropriate or acceptable design. Much of this work is just not considered

extreme anymore. Some of it, in fact, can practically be regarded as mainstream.

Not only does it defy definition, non traditional design defies the rules, conventions and customs of tradition. Non traditional design is a transitory condition, subject to continual change. It is about challenging the status quo and pushing the limits. It provides us with a reflection of the metamorphosis and esthetics of our popular culture. **IT OFFERS US AN ALTERNATIVE WAY OF SEEING AND AN OUTLET FOR SOCIAL COMMENTARY.**

"Less is A Bore"
Robert Venturi

THE DESIGNERS SHOWCASED HERE HAVE CHANGED THE SHAPE AND LOOK OF DESIGN, OFTEN WITH

UNEXPECTED RESULTS. THEIR FRESH APPROACH AVOIDS

TIRED, PREDICTABLE, "SEEN BEFORE" SOLUTIONS. THE DESIGN

ACTIVITY INCLUDED HERE GIVES AN IDEA OF HOW DESIGNERS

TODAY ARE ALTERING SOCIETY'S PERCEPTION OF THEIR

CULTURE AND, IN DOING SO ARE DEFINING TOMORROW'S

MAINSTREAM DESIGN.

"A - What are the boundaries of problems?"
Charles Eames

"Q - What are the boundaries of design?"

WHY DO WE NEED NON TRADITIONAL DESIGN? IT PROVIDES

THE MOMENTUM THAT MOVES US ALONG. BY QUESTIONING

THE WAY THINGS ARE, BY MOVING BEYOND THE ESTABLISHED

RULES, THE NON TRADITIONAL DESIGNER CONTRIBUTES NOT

ONLY TO TODAY, BUT ALSO POINTS THE WAY TO THE NEXT

GENERATION OF DESIGN. WHAT WAS ONCE NON TRADITIONAL AND RULE BREAKING IS ACKNOWLEDGED AS "CUTTING EDGE" AND THEN, BY BECOMING TRADITIONAL OVER TIME, PROVIDES THE SPARK IN THE SEARCH FOR THE NEXT NON TRADITIONAL STYLE. AS A DYNAMIC DESIGN COMMUNITY, WE MUST RECOGNIZE *the contribution of the non traditional designer as being essential to this cycle.*

After going through thousands of entries to develop this book, I realized that making the final selection would not be easy. There are no simple criteria for measuring what is

"ALL DESIGN SHOULD BE NON-TRADITIONAL. OTHERWISE, WHY THE HELL SHOULD WE DO IT?"

Tibor Kalman

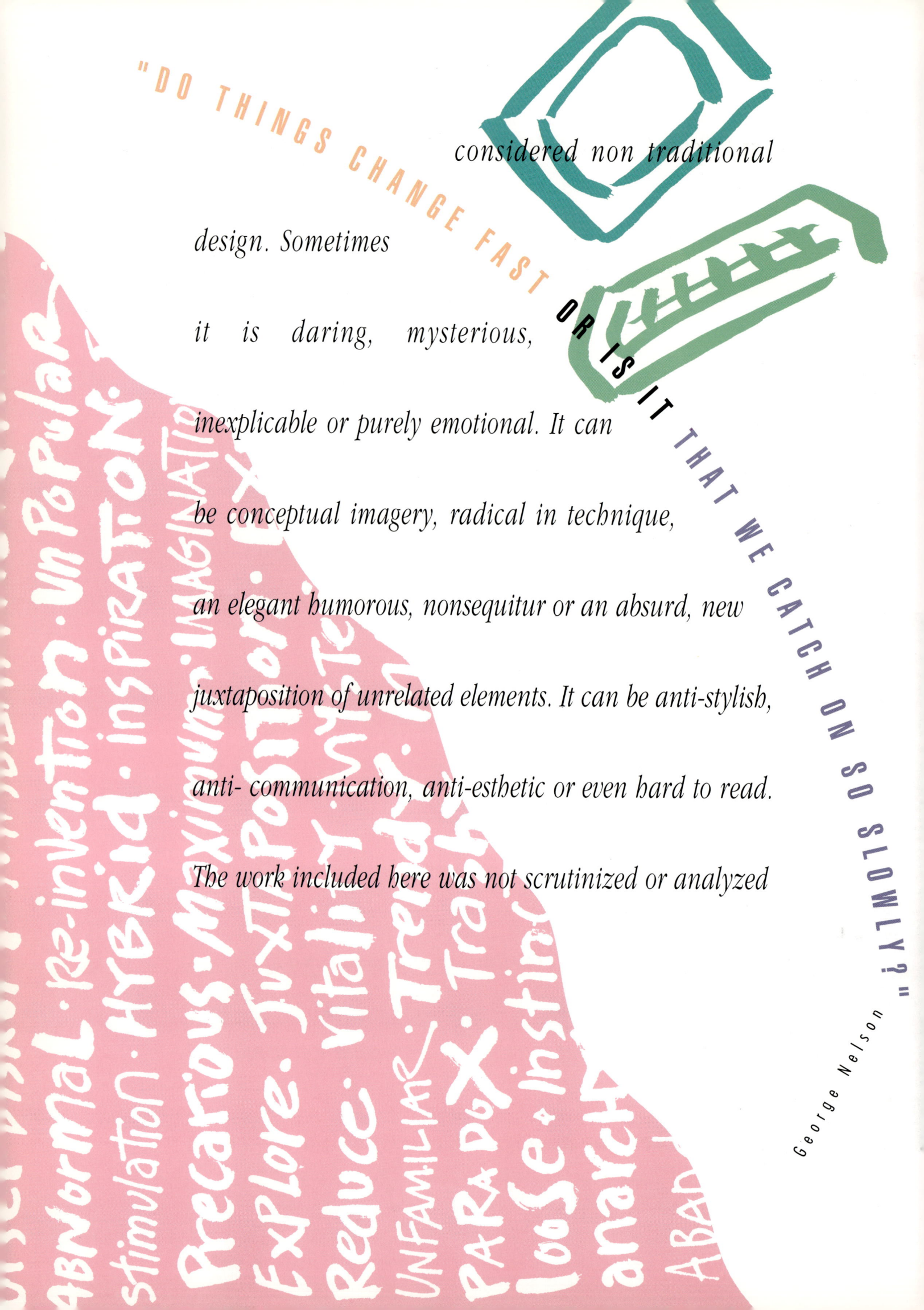

"DO THINGS CHANGE FAST OR IS IT THAT WE CATCH ON SO SLOWLY?"

— George Nelson

considered non traditional design. Sometimes it is daring, mysterious, inexplicable or purely emotional. It can be conceptual imagery, radical in technique, an elegant humorous, nonsequitur or an absurd, new juxtaposition of unrelated elements. It can be anti-stylish, anti-communication, anti-esthetic or even hard to read. The work included here was not scrutinized or analyzed *at length, but was selected for its immediate emotional*

and visual impact.

"I just invent then wait until man comes
around to needing what I've invented."
R. Buckminster Fuller

This ambitious undertaking of assembling such a diverse

and spirited group of graphic design

should be valued for its innovation, imagination and

flexibility. The designs included here came from people I

knew were doing extremely creative

work. It demonstrates to me that

there is a tremendous body of

invigorating and provocative

alternative design being created out

"ALL SERIOUS ART IS AGAINST CONVENTION"

Alexander Liberman

there. It also suggests that there is a lot more to come.

"STYLE is out of FASHION"

This book is about energy, renewal, inspiration and creativity. Enjoy the following pages that contain a sampling of the diverse and inspiring possibilities in the imaginations of

Quentin Crisp

"Change is inevitable since we all become immune to our own experiences."

Milton Glaser

many of today's non traditional designers. I am very much looking forward to the next generation in design, but first, here is an exciting and stimulating portfolio of where we are today.

MIKE QUON
New York City, February 1992

BAM Auction Bidding Kit
Designer
Lynette Cortez
Art Director
Alexander Isley
Design Firm
Alexander Isley Design, New York
Photographer
Monica Stevenson

Isley Architects
"Place and Trace" Template
Designer
Alexander Isley
Design Firm
Alexander Isley Design, New York

Alexander Isley received a B.A. in Environmental Design from the North Carolina State University School of Design and a B.F.A. from the Cooper Union School of Art. He has been a faculty member of the School of Visual Arts in New York, teaching courses in design and typography. He founded Alexander Isley Design in 1988. The firm has a diverse range of clients including MTV, Random House, Giorgio Armani and Brooklyn Academy of Music.

25
BAM
THE 1990
BAM
AUCTION
SCHEDULE
June 26, 1990
6:00 PM
SILENT AUCTION
COCKTAILS AND HORS D'OEUVRES
8:00 PM
Go directly to dance floor for
LIVE AUCTION
With Christie's own
KIMBERLY BAILEY, Auctioneer
Additional comments from
BAM's Official Toastmaster
FRAN LEBOWITZ
8:30 PM
SILENT AUCTION CLOSED
9:00 PM
LIGHT SUPPER
&
DANCING
to the rock, soul and rhythm of
CHRIS THOMAS
NOTE: SEE BACK COVER FOR CONDITIONS OF SALE
Handy official BAM Auction pen; useful for marking your bids. Remove cap before using.
THE OFFICIAL 1990 BAM AUCTION BIDDING NUMBER
25
THE
OFFICIAL
BAM
AUCTION
BIDDING KIT
19
A thoughtfully assembled collection of material designed to facilitate your generosity
90

NIPPON DESIGN CENTER

Typeface Competition
Winners Exhibition
Designer
Kazumasa Nagai
Design Firm
Nippon Design Center, Inc., Tokyo

Kazumasa Nagai left the Sculpture Department at Tokyo National University of Fine Arts and Music and joined Nippon Design Center, Inc. on the occasion of its establishment in 1960. His works are represented in the permanent collections at the Tokyo National Museum of Modern Arts, The Museum of Modern Art in New York as well as many other public museums around the world. He serves as a vice president of Japan Graphic Design Association, is a member of Alliance Graphic International and a member of the Tokyo Art Directors Club.

Communication & Print
Designer
Kazumasa Nagai
Design Firm
Nippon Design Center, Inc., Tokyo

The Exhibition
"Joint Work by
Children 1989"
Designer
Kazumasa Nagai
Design Firm
Nippon Design Center, Inc., Tokyo

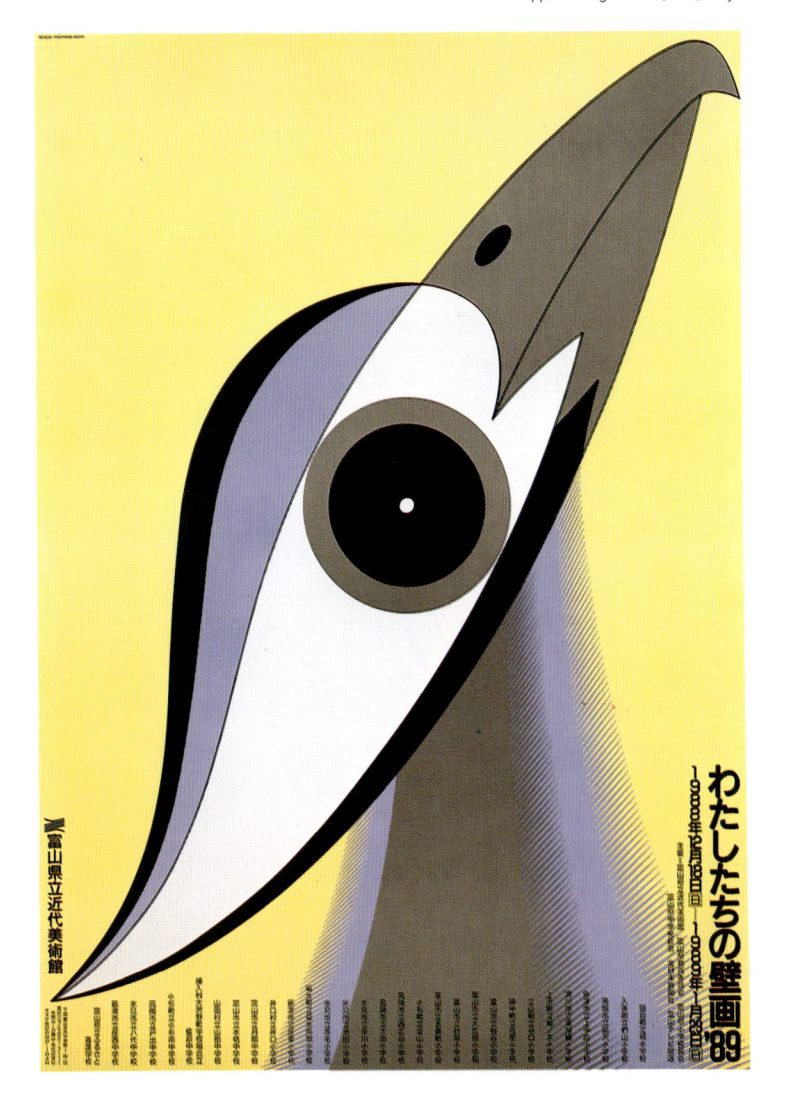

21

The Third International
Poster Triennial
in Toyama, 1991
Designer
Kazumasa Nagai
Design Firm
Nippon Design Center, Inc., Tokyo

Toppan
Designer
Kazumasa Nagai
Design Firm
Nippon Design Center, Inc., Tokyo

NIPPON DESIGN CENTER

THE 3RD INTERNATIONAL POSTER TRIENNIAL IN TOYAMA, 1991
EXHIBITION: July 5th to September 5th, 1991
ORGANIZER SITE: The Museum of Modern Art, Toyama
1-16-12, Nishinakano-machi, Toyama-shi, Japan Tel.0764-21-7111 Fax.0764-22-5996
SUPORTED BY: Japan Graphic designers Association Inc.(JAGDA)
CORPORATION WITH: YKK group/Toppan Printing Co, Ltd.
IPT'91 has been endorsed by icograda-International Council of Graphic Design Associations.
IPT'91
第3回世界ポスタートリエンナーレトヤマ1991
1991年7月5日金—9月5日木
富山県立近代美術館
〒939富山市西中野町1-16-12 TEL.0764(21)7111 FAX.0764(22)5996
IPT'91はicograda国際グラフィックデザイン団体協議会の承認を受けています。
主催=富山県立近代美術館 後援=社団法人 日本グラフィクデザイナー協会(JAGDA) 協力=YKK吉田工業株式会社/凸版印刷株式会社
DESIGN: KAZUMASA NAGAI

C O N C R E T E

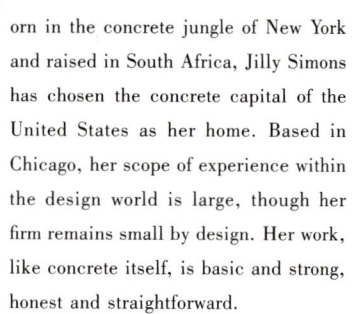

Born in the concrete jungle of New York and raised in South Africa, Jilly Simons has chosen the concrete capital of the United States as her home. Based in Chicago, her scope of experience within the design world is large, though her firm remains small by design. Her work, like concrete itself, is basic and strong, honest and straightforward.

AIGA Conference Dance Card
Designer
Cindy Chang
Design Firm
Concrete, Illinois

"Design is not only an essential means of communication, but also a powerful responsibility."

Marketing/Promotional Brochure
Designers
Jilly Simons and David Robson
Copywriter
Deborah Barron
Design Firm
Concrete, Illinois

Javier Romero was born in Madrid in 1954. In 1977 he founded Grupo Barro, a full-service advertising agency. In 1980 he was awarded a scholarship from the Spanish government to study at the School of Visual Arts in New York. In 1982 he founded Periscope, Inc., a design firm. In 1985 he founded Javier Romero Design, Inc. in New York. He has taught at Parsons School of Design and School of Visual Arts. His work has been featured in the books *Designing With Illustration* and *Promo* and in design magazines in the USA, Spain, France, Switzerland, Japan and Korea. This year he will be launching unique designer ties for the European and American markets.

Art Direction
Magazine Cover
Designer
Javier Romero
Design Firm
Javier Romero Design, Inc.,
New York

Human Rights Now!
Designer
Javier Romero
Design Firm
Javier Romero Design, Inc.,
New York

27

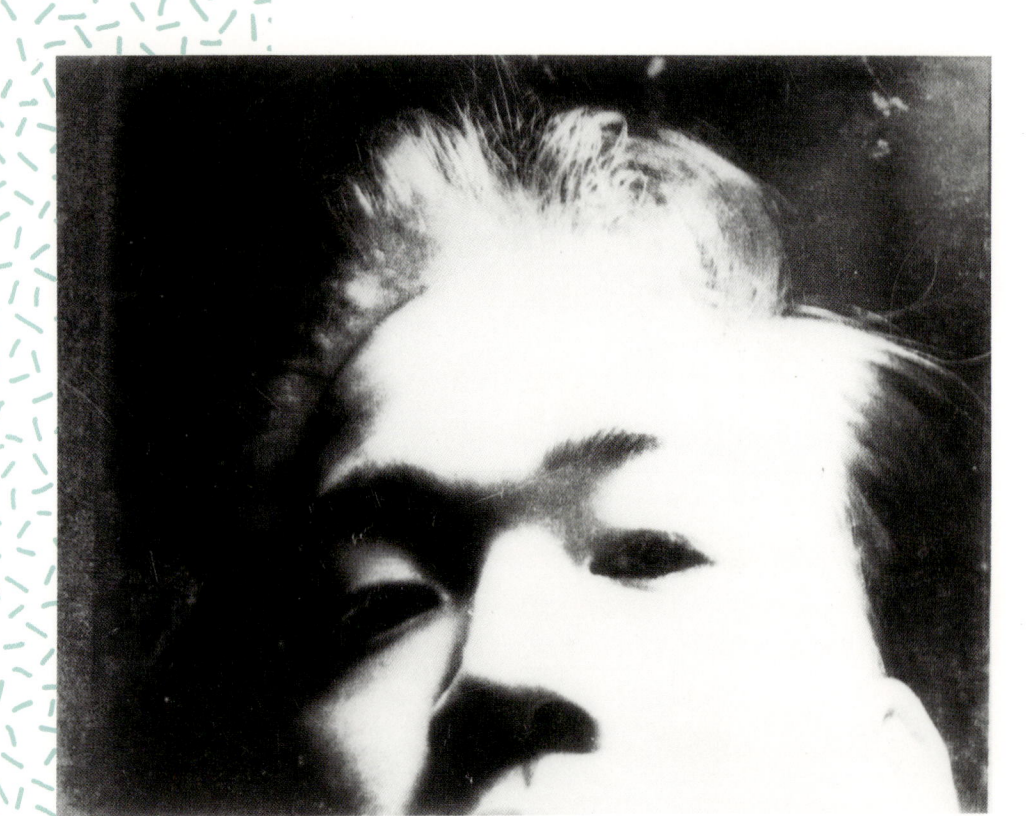

Yoko Ono: The Bronze Age
Designer
Allen Hori, Student,
Cranbrook Academy of Art

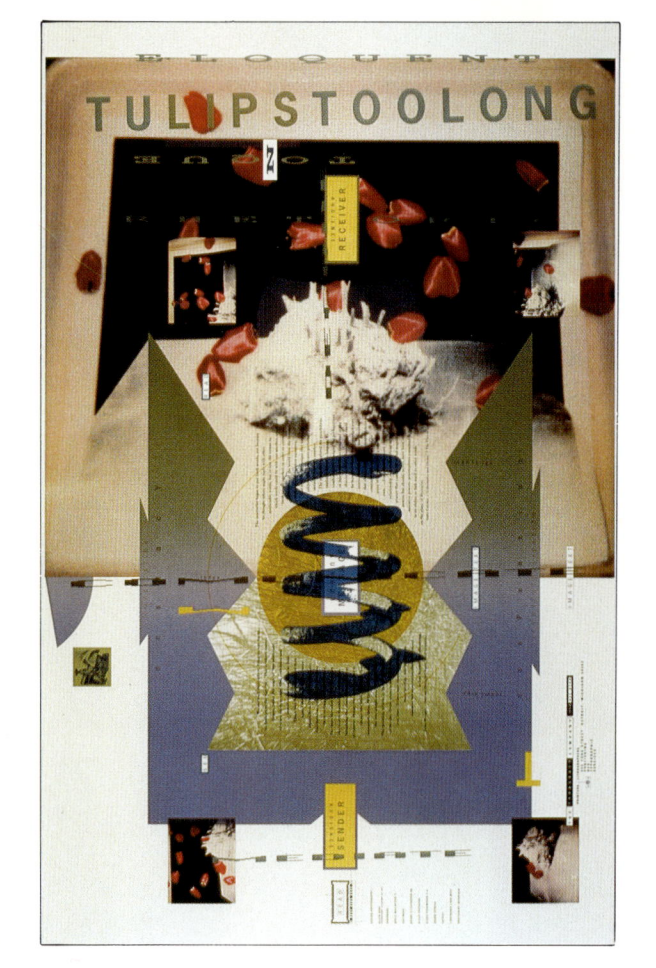

Tulipstoolong
Designer
Allen Hori, Student,
Cranbrook Academy of Art

DIAS P NTS TWO EV INGS WIT
CRANBROOK PRESENTS
yoko ono
yoko ono
SEPTEMBER 28 AND 29 AT 7:45PM
SEPTEMBER 23toOCTOBER 29, 1989
AFRICA CENTER
ART CENTER
38 KING ST.
500 LONE PINE ROAD
LONDON WC2
BLOOMFIELD HILLS, MI
TEL. BAY 9409
TEL. 313.645.3323
THE BRONZE AGE
YOKO ONO
CRANBROOK ART MUSEUM
The Bronze Age
Poster designed by Yoko Ono
Curated by Jon Hendricks

Rupture Sutural
Designer
Allen Hori, Student,
Cranbrook Academy of Art

ALLEN HORI

31

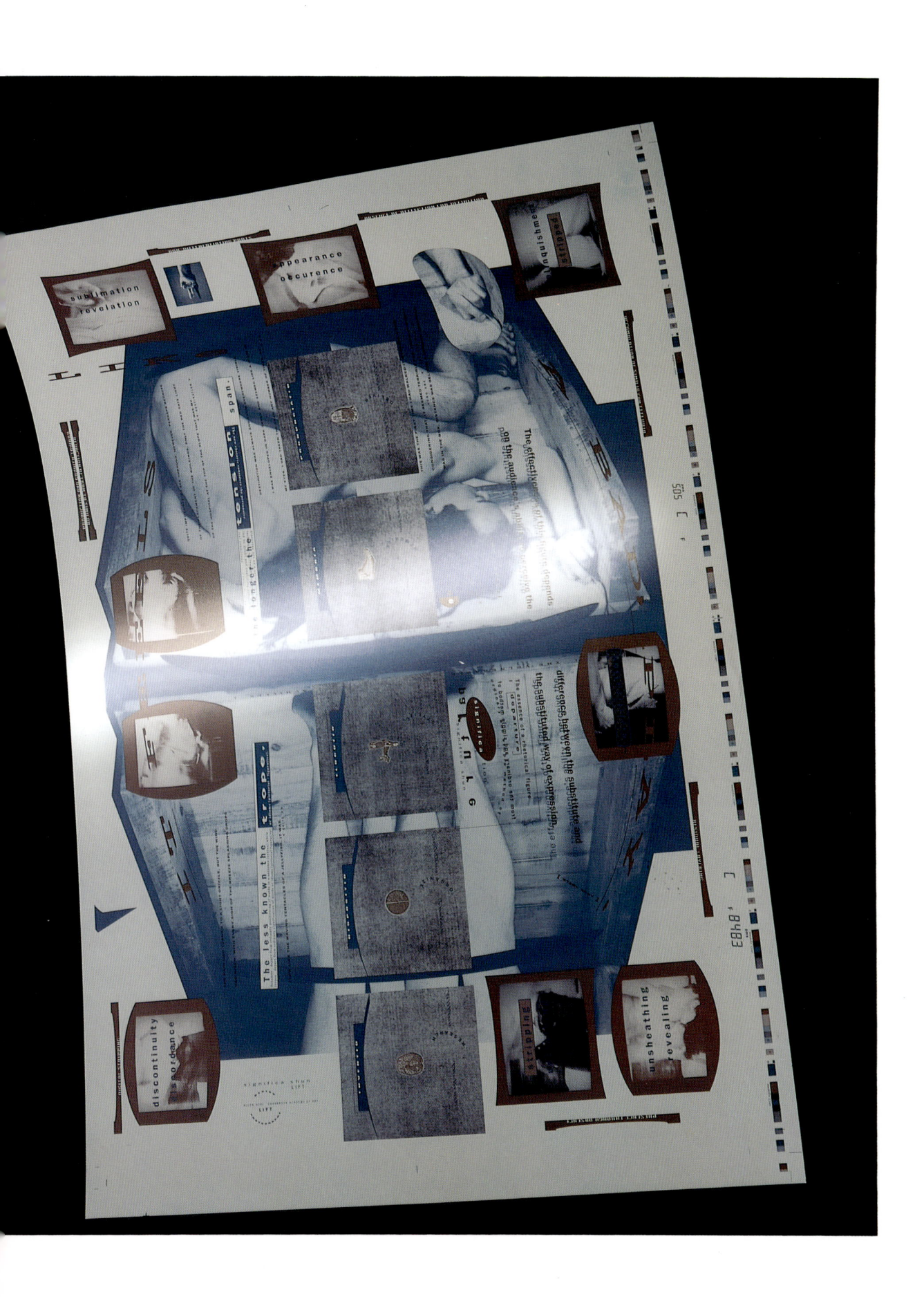

Cover Design
The Rocket Magazine
Designer
Jesse Reyes
Photographer
Kevin Westenberg
© 1988 The Rocket Magazine/
Jesse Reyes Graphic Design

A Seattle native born of Anglo-Bulgarian and Filipino parents, Jesse Reyes has "about as non-traditional an origin as it gets." After studying painting and illustration at the University of Washington, Reyes saw a poster design for a theatre company's production of *The Adding Machine* done by Art Chantry. "The Design was so distinctive and powerful that I decided right then and there that graphic design was what I wanted to do." Reyes transferred to Seattle Central Community College and finished near the top of his graduating class. Later he took a course at The New School of Visual Concepts in order to meet Chantry. In the ensuing nine years, Reyes has been a freelance designer for theater groups and various small clients, a designer for a municipal authority, and an art director of the influential Seattle pop culture magazine *The Rocket*. Since 1989 he has been Design Director of the New York City-based music publication *Guitar World* and concurrently since 1991 an editor/publication designer for Harris Comics.

"*If I was screwed-up going into that (Chantry's) class, Art's influence made the effect permanent. Art turned me on to a lot of resources that I hadn't been aware of in any detail previously: Dada, the Russian avant-garde, the Bauhaus, American Depression-era designers like Lester Beall and Bradbury Thompson and such. Add to that my own interests in the pop culture that I had grown up with in the '60s and '70s—like monster magazines and comic books and rock bands—then you pretty much have the intellectual basis for my approach to design.*"

Feature Design
Guitar World Magazine
Designer
Jesse Reyes
Design Firm
Guitar World Magazine Art Dept.,
New York
Photographers
Pat Blashill, Rick Olivier
and Kevin Westenberg
© 1991 Harris Publications

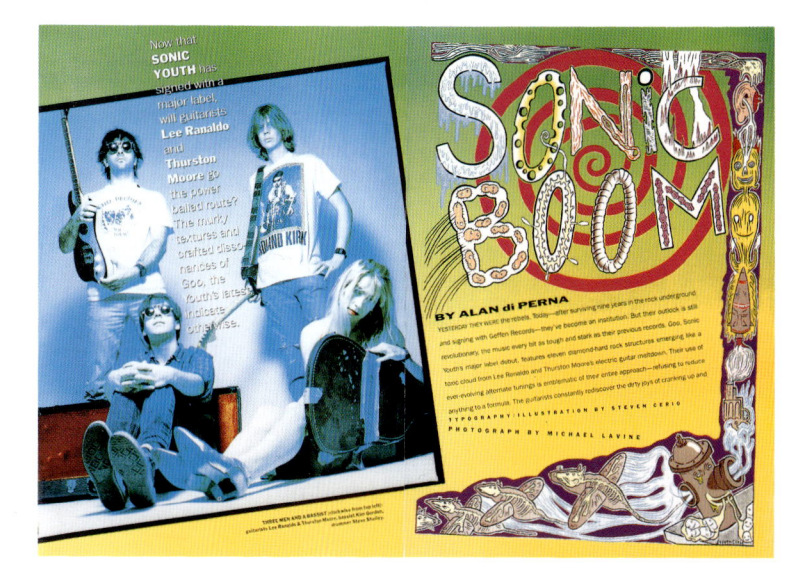

Feature Design
Guitar World Magazine
Designer
Jesse Reyes
Design Firm
Guitar World Magazine Art Dept.,
New York
Photographers
Pat Blashill, Rick Olivier
and Kevin Westenberg
© 1991 Harris Publications

Feature Design
Guitar World Magazine
Designer
Jesse Reyes
Artist
Steven Cerio
Design Firm
Guitar World Magazine Art Dept.,
New York
Photographer
Michael Lavine
© 1990 Harris Publications

33

WELLER INSTITUTE FOR THE CURE OF DESIGN

*d*on Weller is the founder of the Weller Institute for the Cure of Design. He went to Washington State University where he took the foundation courses for a career in veterinary medicine and ended up with a B.A. in Fine Art. He worked for various design firms in Los Angeles until he opened his own office in 1968. Since 1973 Don's partner in business has been the talented Chikako, who became his wife. After moving back and forth between New York and Los Angeles he has finally settled down in Park City, Utah.

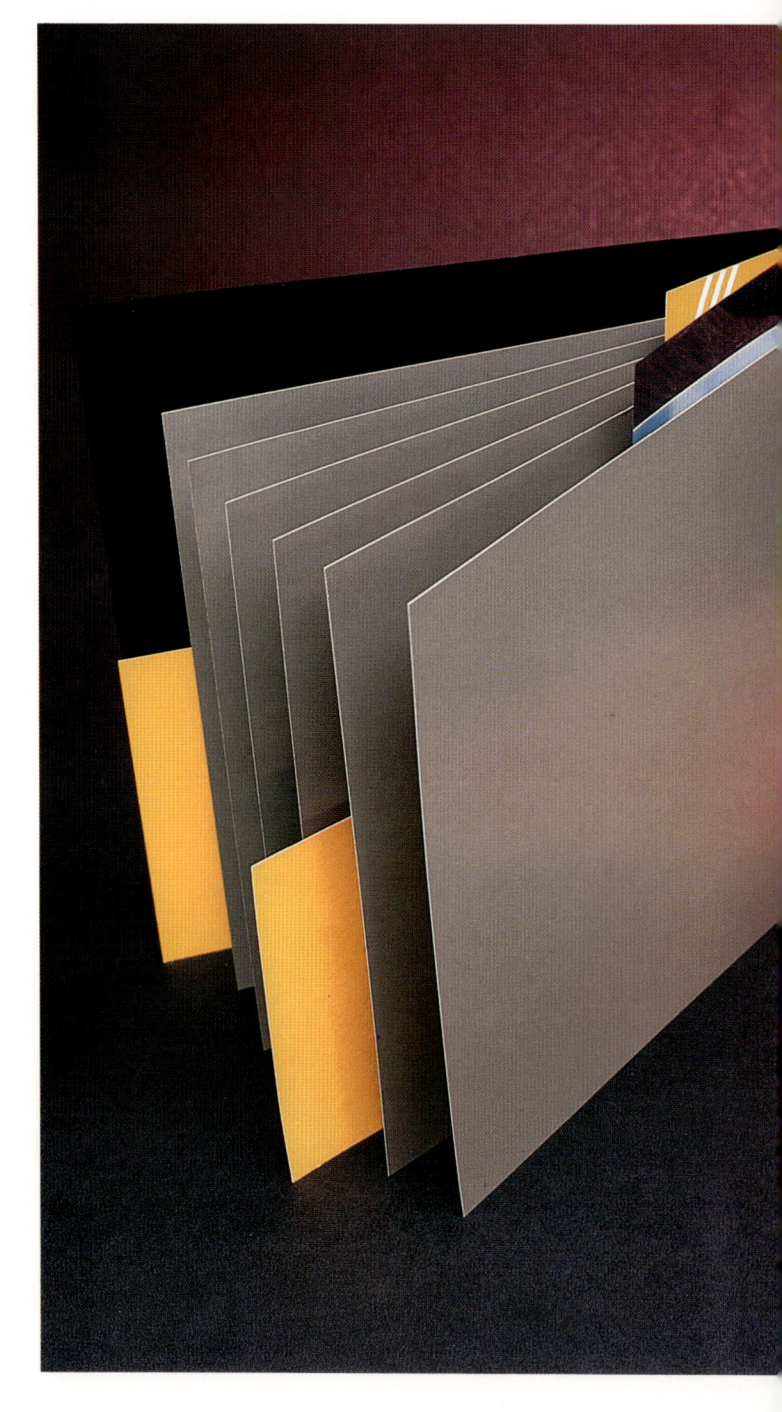

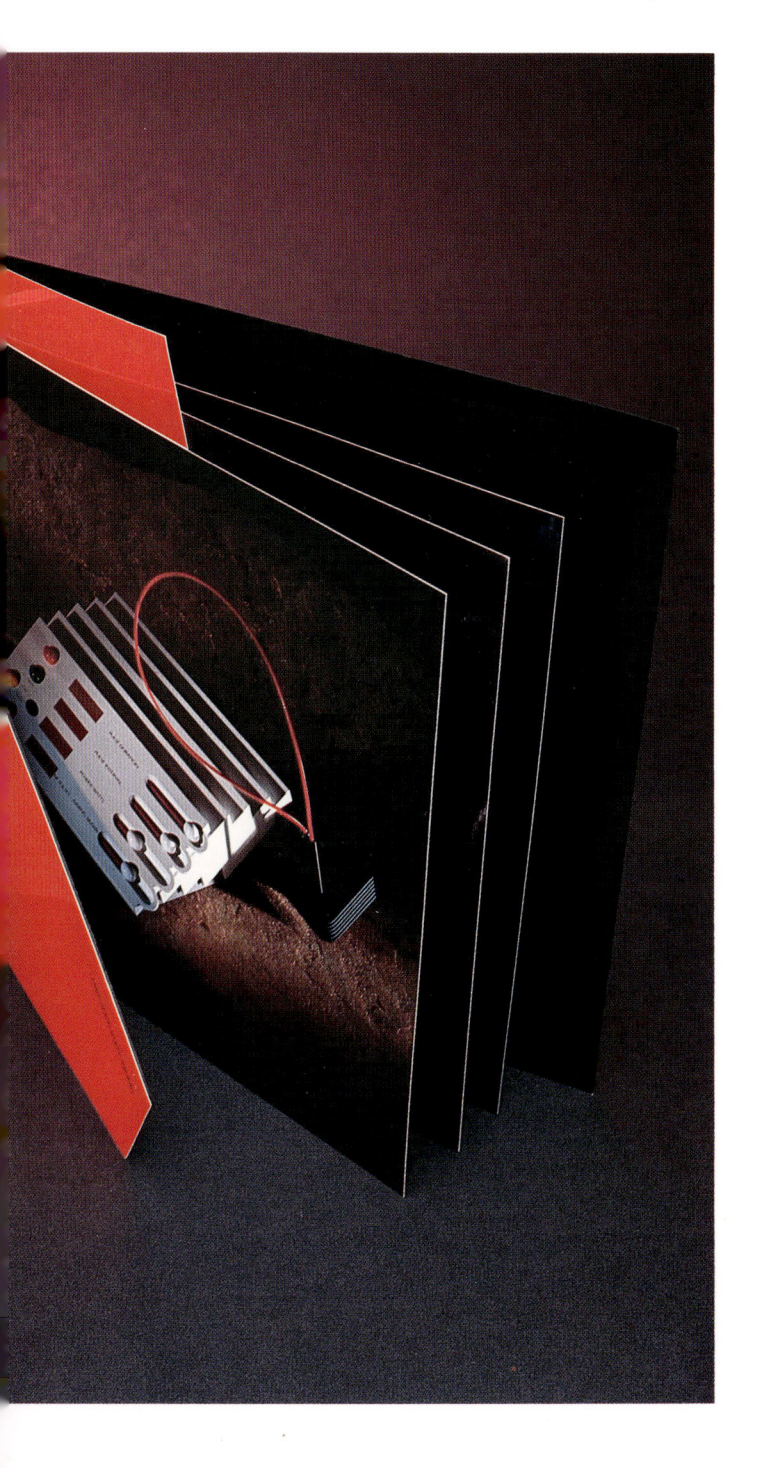

IDA Brochure
Designer
Don Weller
Design Firm
Weller Institute
for the Cure of Design

"To ignore tradition is short sighted. But stepping beyond tradition and taking a chance is where the fun lies for a designer and his audience. The step to the unexpected is what keeps the work fresh."

"*I am fascinated by the human condition. We manage to entangle ourselves in everything from wars to love and expect to leave a record of activity for future humans to learn from. The history books don't recount any lessening of these foibles so I've questioned whether our lives are any different or more meaningful from centuries past.*"

nationally recognized in Canada for the last ten years, Derrick Carter's Studio, HotHouse Visual Room, is often cited as one of the most curious in Canada. He has received attention from several publications including *Graphis* and *I.D. Magazine*, and participated in exhibitions in North America, Germany and Japan.

Reconstruction of
Homo Sapiens A
Designers
Derrick Carter and Mark Murphy
Design Firm
Hot House, Vancouver, B. C.

Icograda Montreal 1991
Business Convergence
Designers
Derrick Carter and Mark Murphy
Design Firm
Hot House, Vancouver, B. C.

Business Convergence
Convergence économique

icograda montréal 1991

The 14th Congress of ICOGRADA, International Council of Graphic Design Associations
Le 14ᵉ congrès ICOGRADA, Conseil international des associations de design graphique

GRANARY BOOKS

Born in Copenhagen, Denmark, Henrik Drescher moved to the United States in his teens. Having no formal art training, he asserts that "plenty of travel" facilitated the launching of his career as a non-traditional artist. He attempts to let his designs develop spontaneously from "seeds" such as randomly found objects and distorted images.

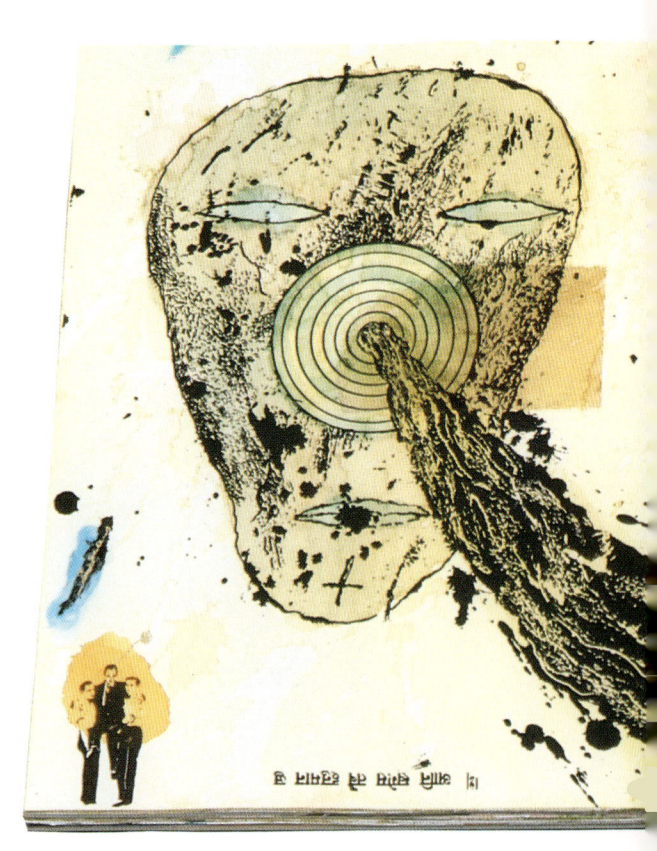

"My aim is to reach the place…the mind's eye, where pictures are felt and tasted, rather than processed by linear thought and logic."

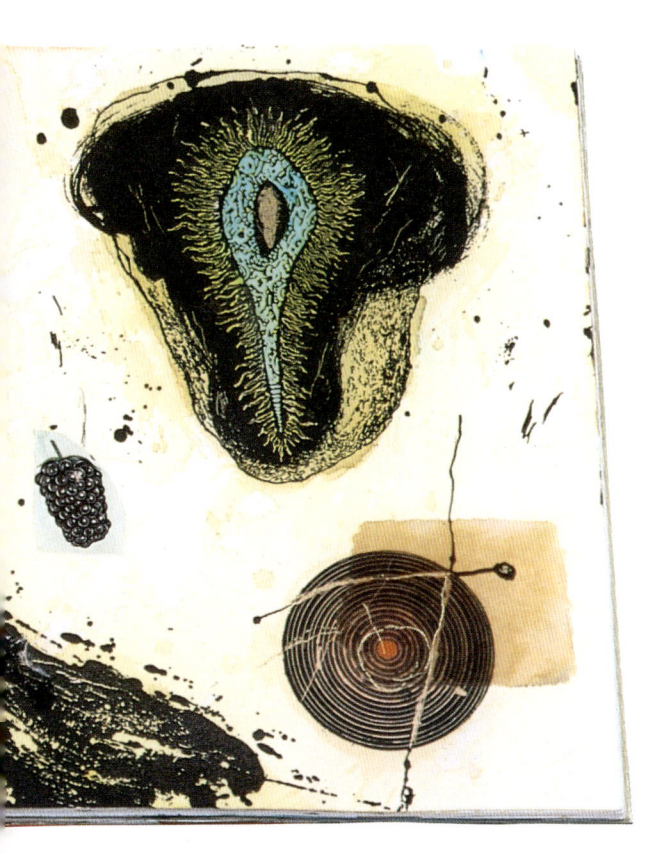

"Too Much Bliss"
Designer
Henrik Drescher
Design Firm
Granary Books

Entertainment Totem
of Universal's City Walk
Designers
Bob Bangham and Charles White III
Design Firm
Olio, California
Photographer
Richard Hines

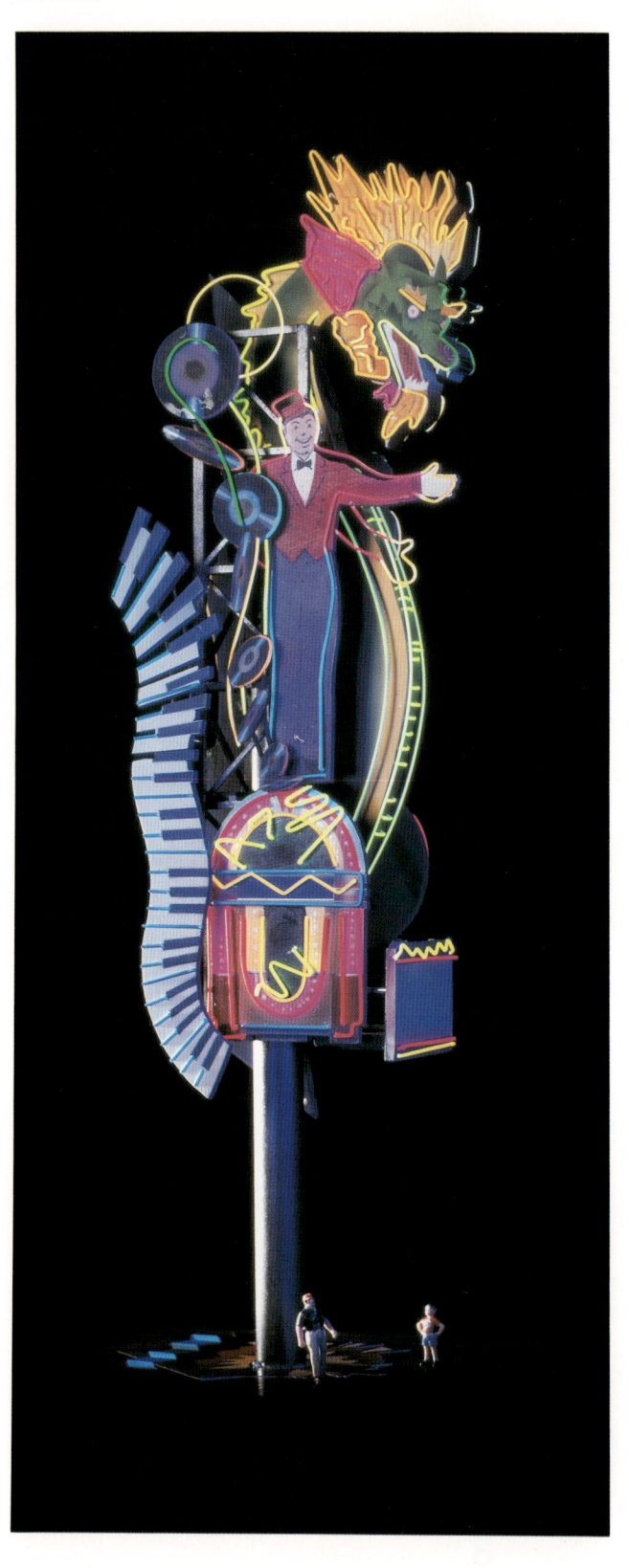

After studying at Art Center College of Design, Charles White III, started his own design studio in 1964. He later moved to New York City and established himself as an important illustrator whose work with the airbrush has become legendary. He returned to Los Angeles in 1976 and in 1980 started the influential Willardson + White illustration studio with fellow airbrush artist, Dave Willardson. His versatile career includes credits in animation film, set design, trade/fine art shows, and illustration. In 1991, White founded Olio, a collaborative of graphic artists, set designers, architects, writers, and fine artists. Olio projects include Tokyo Disney, MCA City Walk and Treasure Island at the Mirage.

After earning a bachelors degree in design from Clemson University, Bob Bangham went on to complete his Masters of Architecture at The Southern California Institute of Architecture. Over the last 10 years, he has worked for innovative architectural firms as well as doing his own architecture and illustration projects. Since their meeting in 1988, he and Charles White have worked together on several large-scale projects.

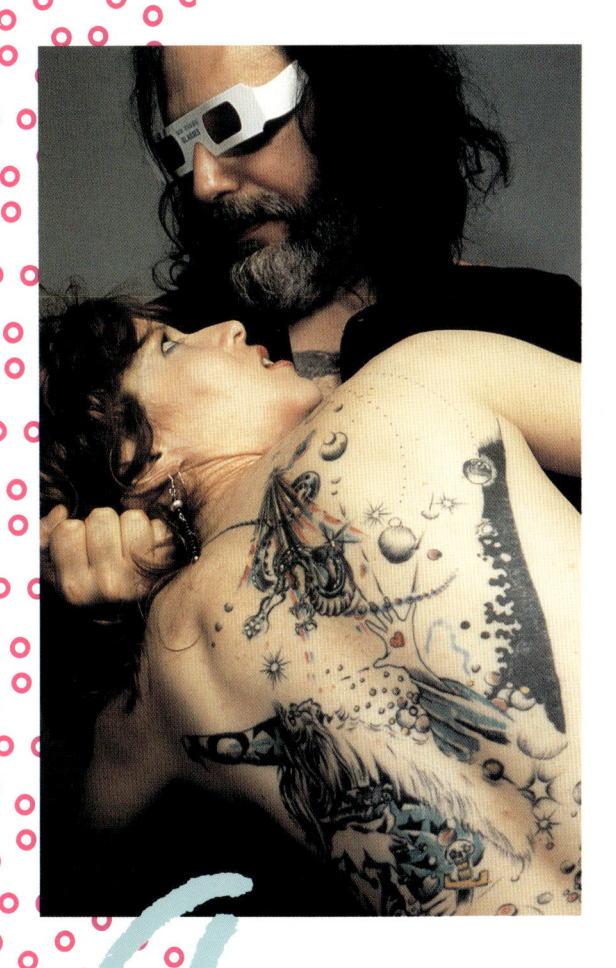

a recognized artist for more than 30 years, Spider Webb ("The Eight-Legged One") is the most well known tattooist in the world. He is a graduate of the School of Visual Arts, holds a Maestro En Bellas Artes from Instituto Allende and a PhD in Philosophy from Yale University. He is a performance artist as well as a multi media artist, and has been the forerunner of the exploding popularity of tattoo art. He was the first to display flash art in galleries and museums and was the original organizer of a convention for tattoo artists. His work has been shown in museums including the Art Institute of Chicago, the Louvre in Paris, the Boston Museum of Fine Arts as well as the Brooklyn Museum and Detroit Institute of the Arts.

Leopard Tattoo
Designer
Spider Webb
Design Firm
Spider Webb Studios, Connecticut
Photographer
Jean-Marie Guyaux
© *Spider Webb Studios*

PAUL DAVIS

Paul Davis Exhibition
Designer
Paul Davis
Creative Director
Silas Rhodes
Design Firm
Paul Davis Studio, New York

Paul Davis was born and raised in Oklahoma and attended the School of Visual Arts in New York on an Art Awards scholarship from *Scholastic* magazine. Since the early 1960s, his work has appeared on the pages and covers of many major magazines in the United States and abroad, and on book jackets, record albums, posters, and films. Books devoted to his work include E.P. Dutton's *Paul Davis Posters and Paintings*, and *Paul Davis/Faces* published by Friendly Press, and *The Arcadia Seasonal Mural and Cookbook* published by Harry Abrams, Inc. which features a fold-out reproduction of a 70-foot wrap-around mural he created for New York's Arcadia Restaurant.

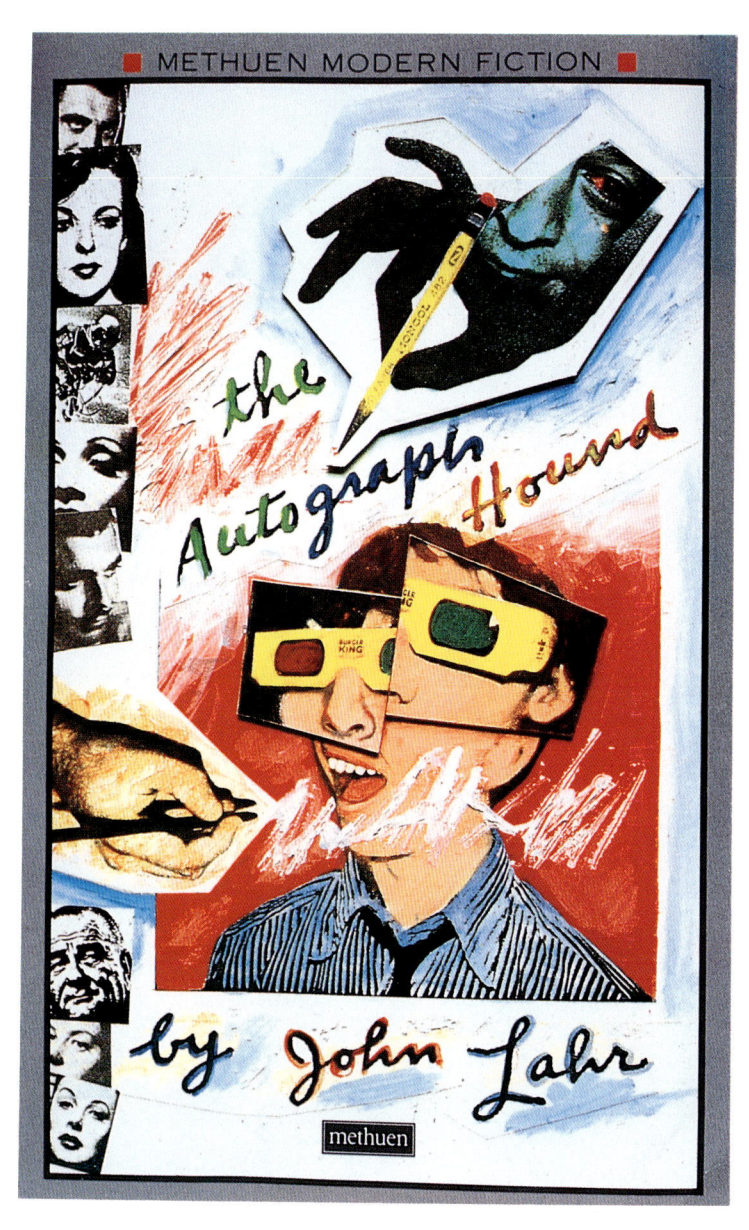

The Autograph Hound
Designer
Paul Davis
Illustrator
Paul Davis
Design Firm
Paul Davis Studio, New York

Normal Magazine
Designer
Paul Davis
Illustrator
Paul Davis
Design Firm
Paul Davis Studio, New York

43

Wigwag Magazine,
September 1990
Designer
Risa Zaitschek
Illustrator
Maira Kalman
Design Firm
Paul Davis Studio, New York

Wigwag Magazine,
May 1990
Designer
Risa Zaitschek
Illustrator
J. Otto Siebold
Design Firm
Paul Davis Studio, New York

PAUL DAVIS

WIGWAG

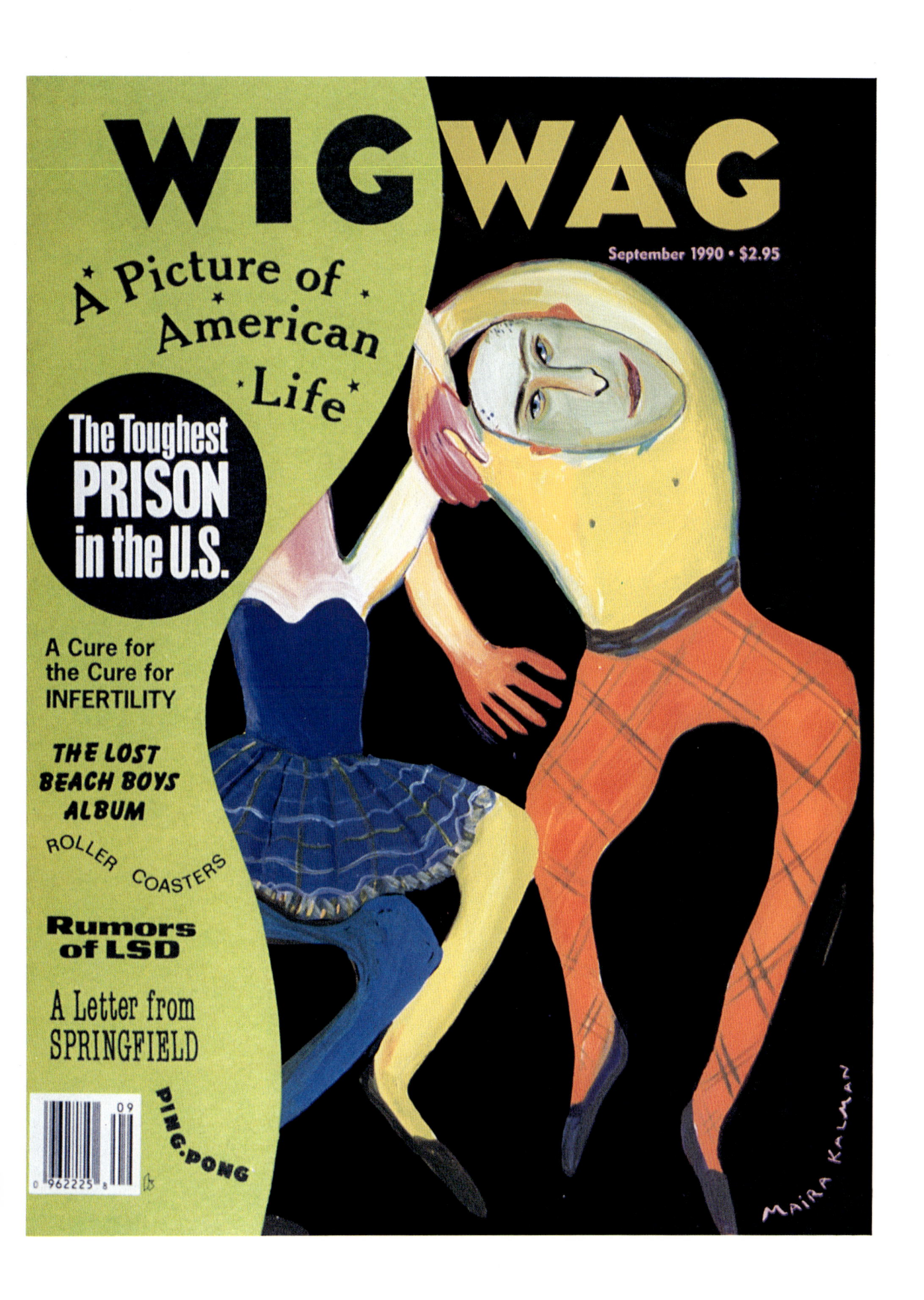

September 1990 • $2.95

A Picture of American Life

The Toughest PRISON in the U.S.

A Cure for the Cure for INFERTILITY

THE LOST BEACH BOYS ALBUM

ROLLER COASTERS

Rumors of LSD

A Letter from SPRINGFIELD

PING-PONG

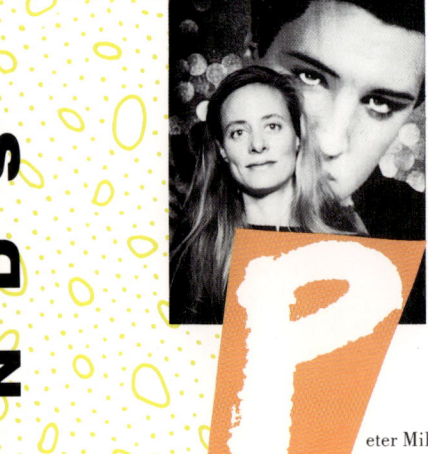

COREY EDMONDS MILLEN

Peter Millen was born and trained in England and began his career in the music industry and theater promotion.

Robyn Ewing began work as a fashion editor, later worked as an illustrator and finally an editorial designer. She currently works at Scholastic Inc. having immense fun with type.

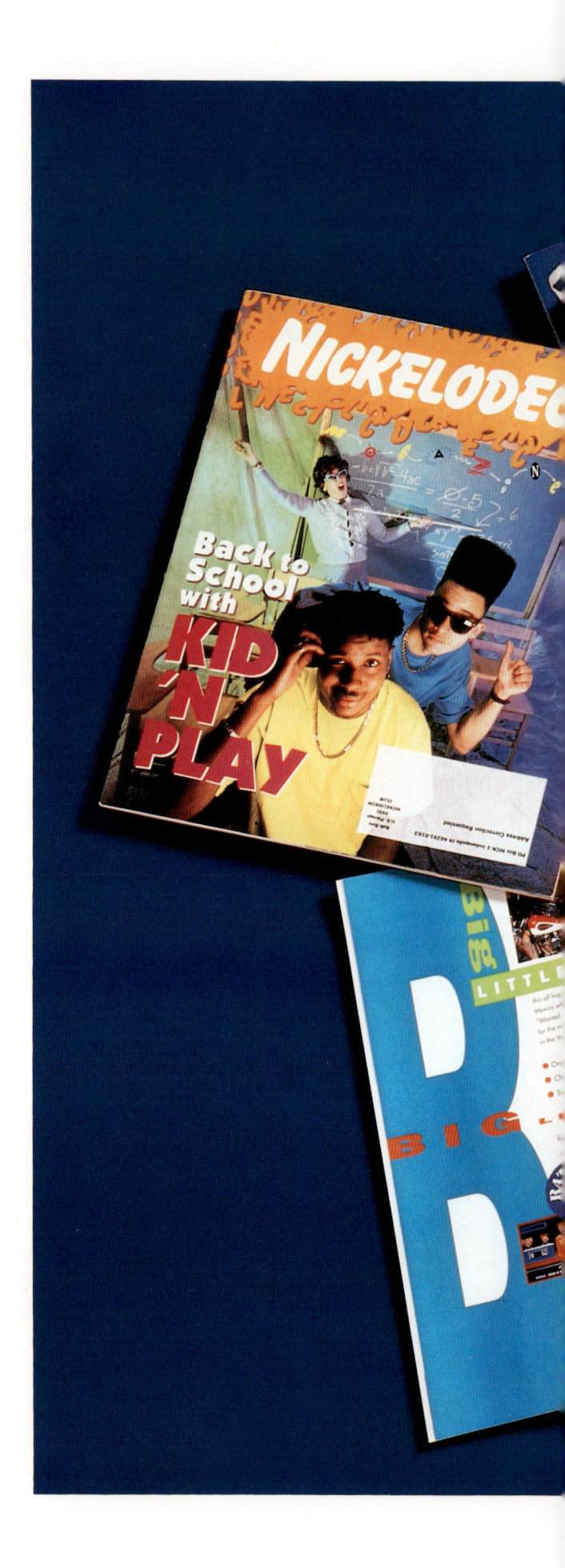

Nickelodeon Magazine
Designers
Robin Ewing and Peter Millen
Design Firm
Corey Edmonds Millen, New York
Photographer
Russell French

Promotion for Photographer
Graham Haber
Designers
Wing Chan and Graham Haber
Art Director
Wing Chan
Copywriter
Richard Mann
Design Firm
Wing Chan Design, New York
Photographer
Graham Haber

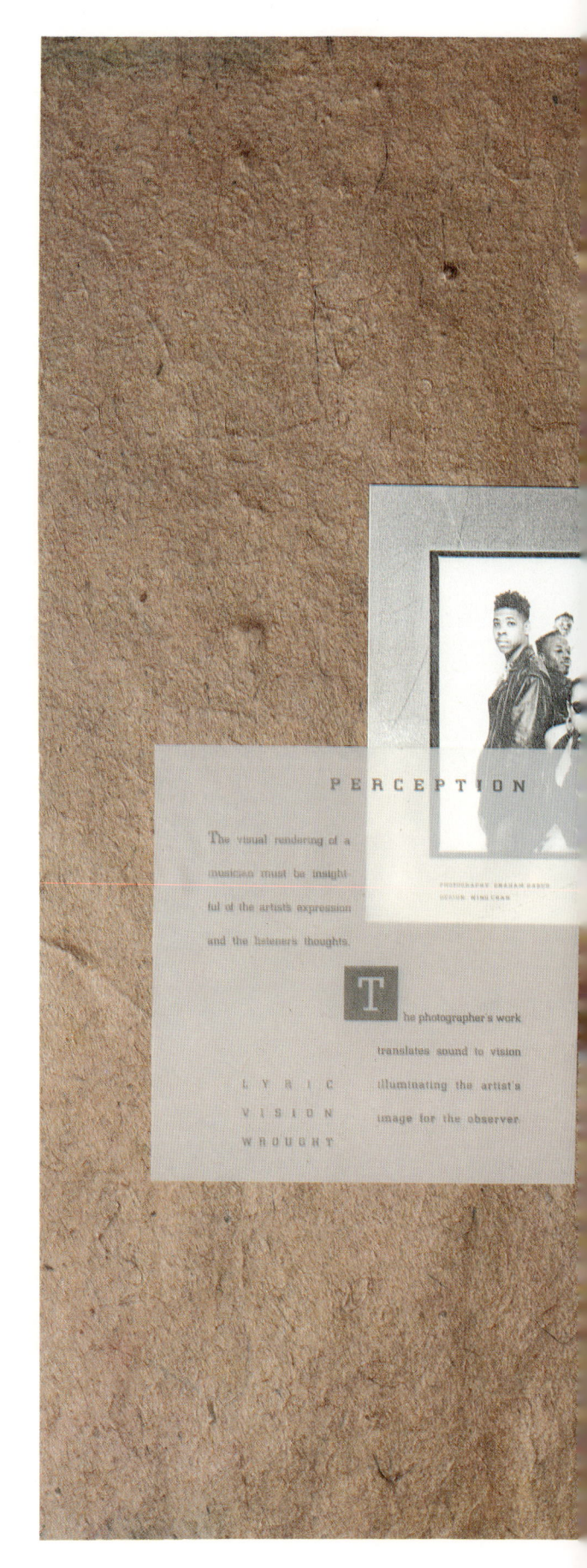

49

The director of an animation studio, the Ink Tank, R.O. Blechman pursues a simultaneous career as an illustrator. His illustrations have appeared in most major magazines, and have been exhibited in galleries in New York, Paris, Berlin and Munich. In 1984 his animated version of Igor Stravinsky's "The Soldier's Tale" was released for public television, and won an Emmy Award for "Outstanding Individual Achievement."

Christmas Card
Designer
R.O. Blechman
Artist
Isabelle Dervaux
Design Firm
The Ink Tank, New York
© 1987 The Ink Tank

51

Double Your Pleasure
Designer
Rick Valicenti
Design Firm
THIRST, Illinois

Rick Valicenti's company, Thirst, follows three essential commandments: first, acknowledge the process of design; second; accept that all business is about creating versions of reality; and third, make self-expression evident in every job. The result, Valicenti claims, is "art with function."

Modern Design 1991
(2 Sided Poster)
Designer
Rick Valicenti
Design Firm
THIRST, Illinois
Photographer
Corinne Pfister and Michael Pappas

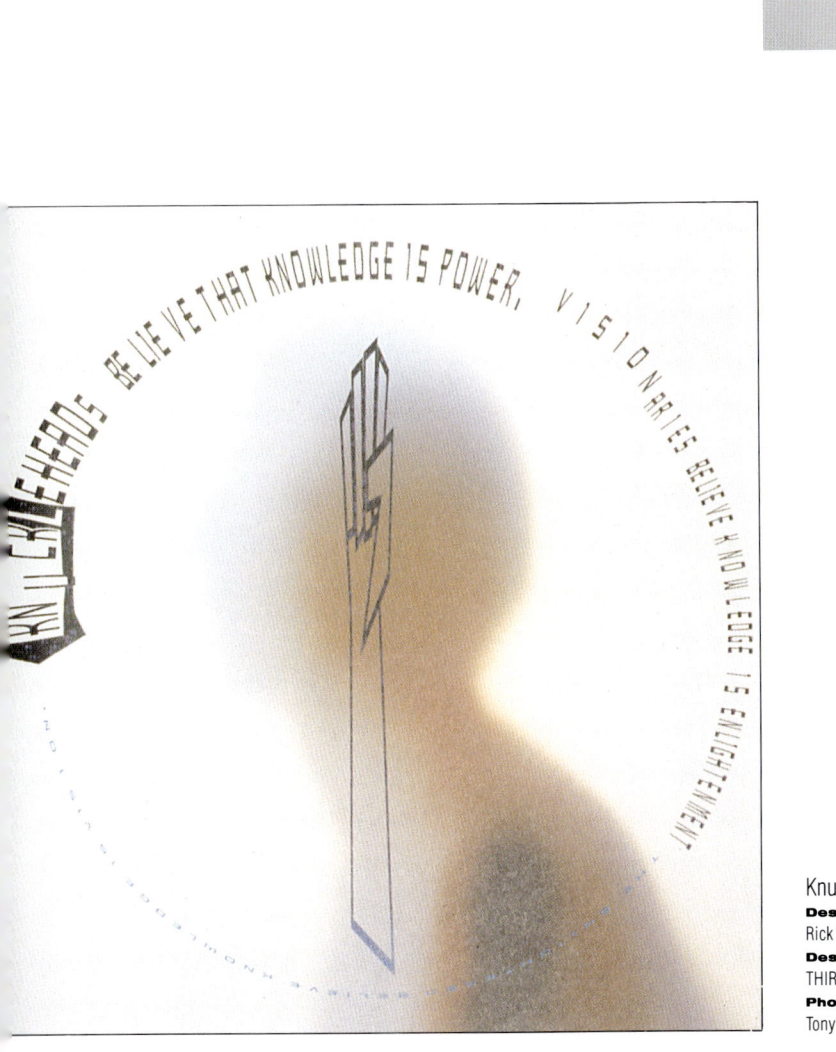

Knucklehead
Designer
Rick Valicenti
Design Firm
THIRST, Illinois
Photographer
Tony Klassen

53

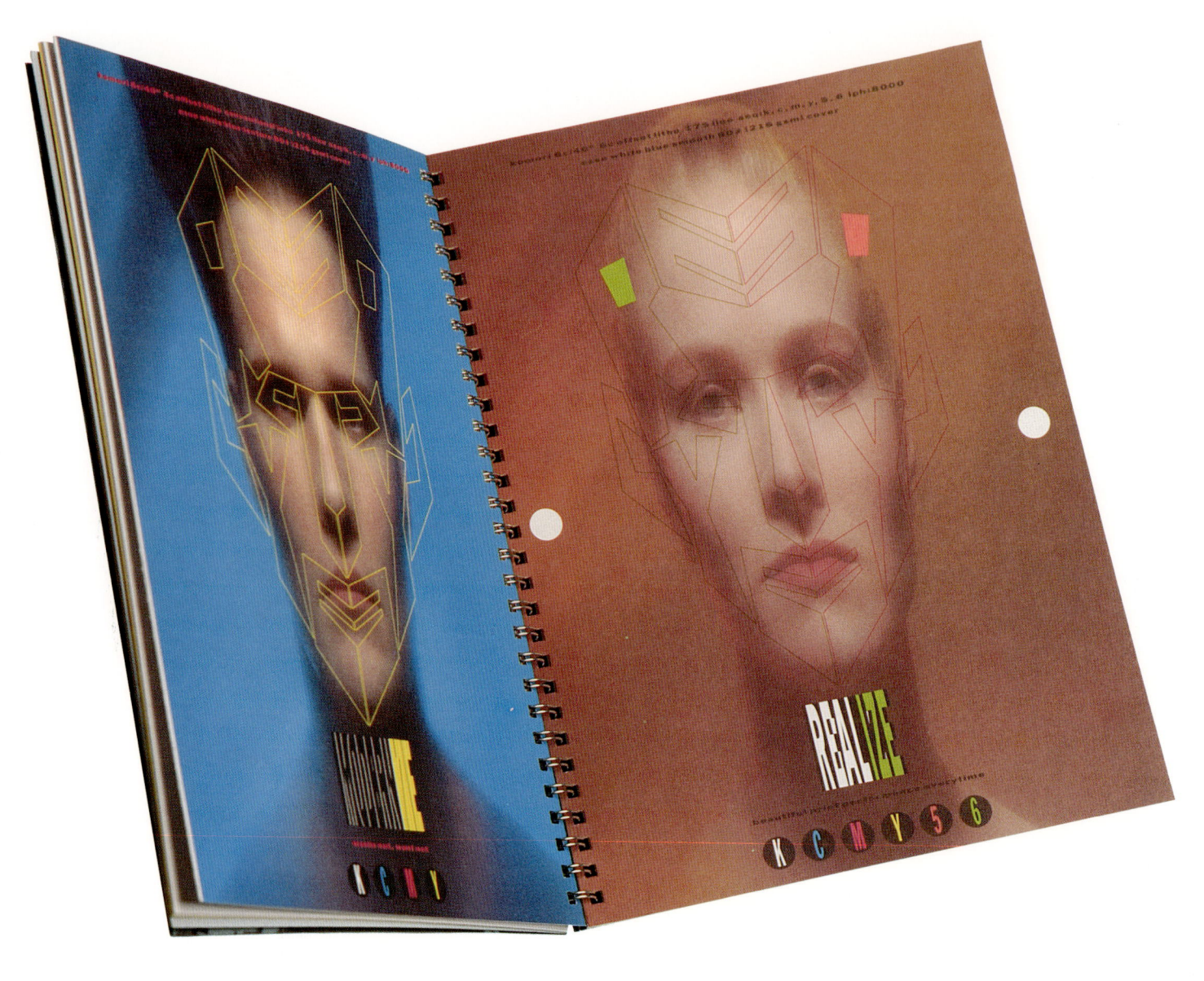

The IZE Have It
Designer
Rick Valicenti
Production
Michael Giammanco
Design Firm
THIRST, Illinois
Photographers
Corinne Pfister and Michael Pappas

T H I R S T

Gilbert International
Communique
Designer
Rick Valicenti
Production
Michael Giammanco
Design Firm
THIRST, Illinois
Photographer
Tony Klassen

55

Push! Magazine Cover
Designers
Giovanni Russo and Lloyd Ziff
Design Firm
Lloyd Ziff Design Group, Inc.,
New York
Photographer
Edward Ruscha

Lloyd Ziff, recognized for his innovative creativity and extensive background within the magazine industry, founded the Lloyd Ziff Design Group, Inc. a graphic design studio, in 1988. Previously, he was the Art Director responsible for the launch of numerous prestigious national magazines: *New West*, *Vanity Fair*, *Conde Nast Traveler*, and the redesign and repositioning of *House & Garden*. Ziff is also an accomplished photographer and teacher. His photographs have been featured in several magazines including *Interview*, *Arts & Architecture*, *GQ*, *Rolling Stone*, *New West*, and *House & Garden*. Since 1983 Lloyd has been teaching at Parsons School of Design.

Double Page Ad
For Parfum BIC
Designer
Lloyd Ziff
Design Firm
Lloyd Ziff Design Group, Inc.,
New York
Photographers
Edward Addeo
and Jeanette Beckman

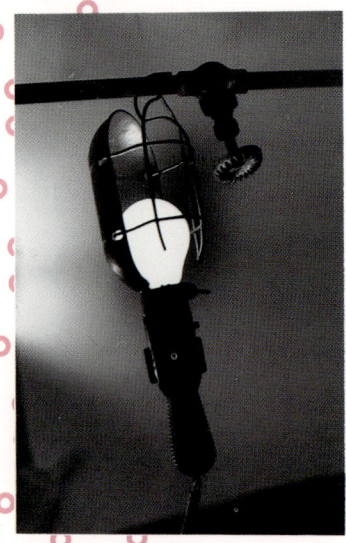

"*I prefer to allow design to act as an expression of the times we are living in; to operate as a cultural generalist, observing as I am executing a design. In this way I am able to develop formal and conceptual directions as I am working, turning visual accidents into assets.*"

"Het Boek"
Designer
Scott Santoro
Design Firm
Worksight

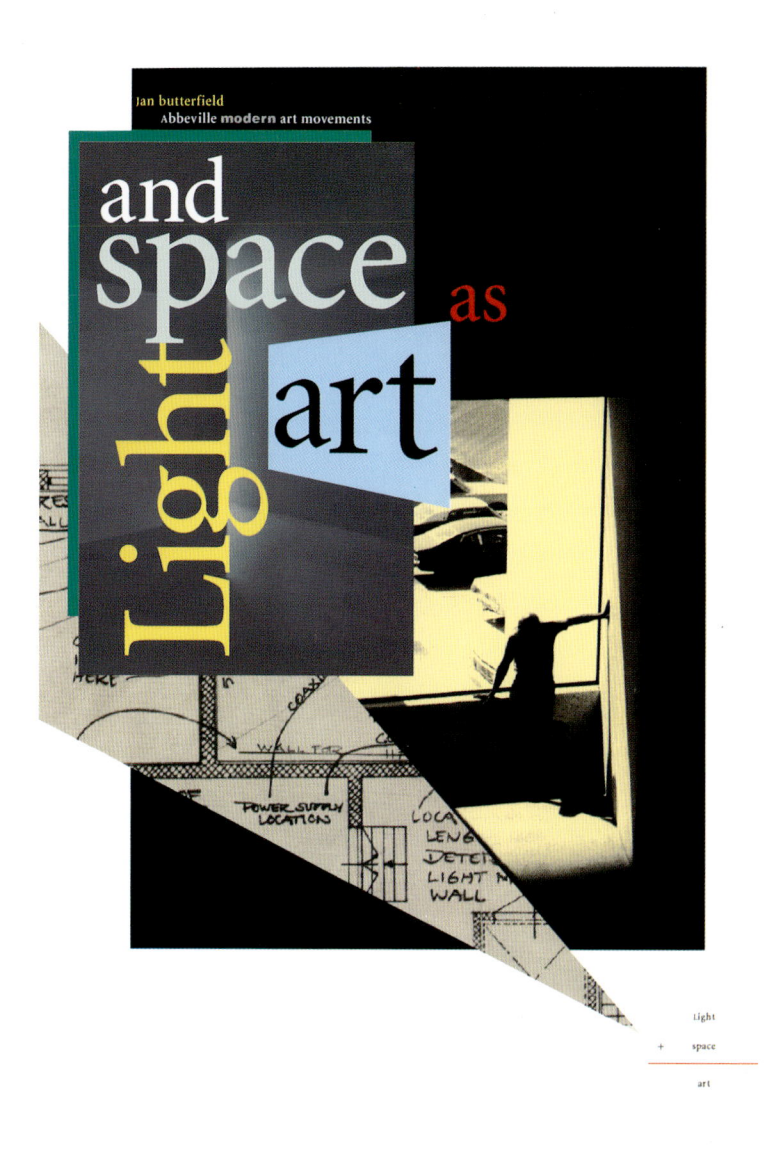

"Light and Space As Art"
Designer
Scott Santoro
Design Firm
Worksight

Input—For What
We Are About to Receive
Designer
Scott Santoro
Design Firm
Worksight

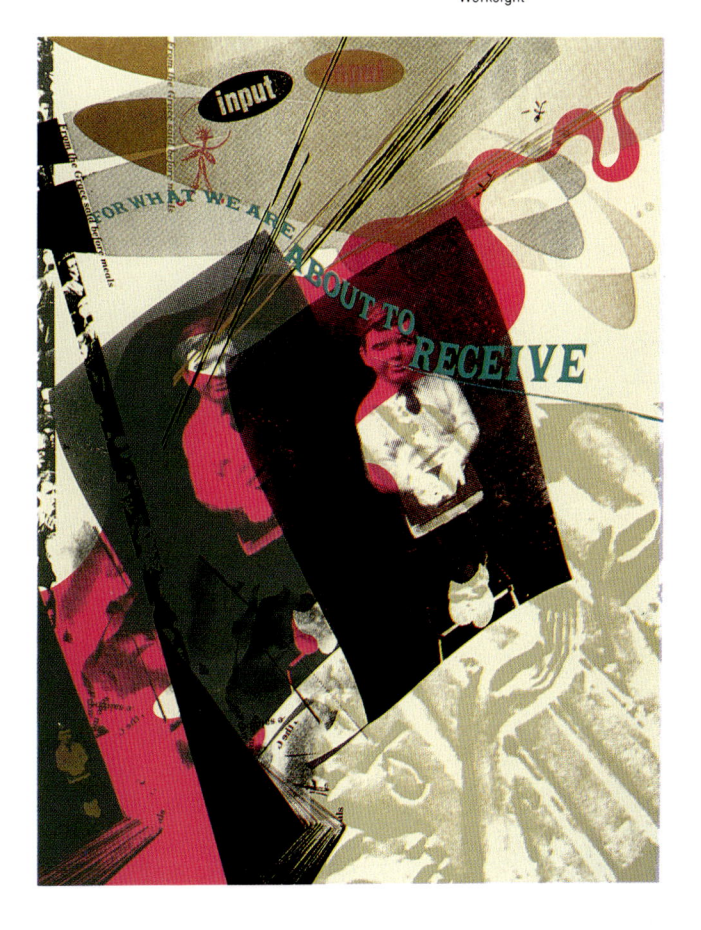

PAPER MOON GRAPHICS

Robert Fitch failed illustration during all four of his years at Tyler School of Design in Philadelphia, because he says he "never completed an illustration." Undaunted, he continued to take the course to help himself develop a sense of conceptual design. He left Philadelphia in the snow and went to Los Angeles where he discovered the newly formed firm we now know as Papermoon Graphics. He liked what he saw in their line, because as he says, "I didn't know any better." Soon after, he began working there and has been with Papermoon ever since.

After attending Otis/Parsons and Art Center College of Design, Patrick James has gone on to work in a number of different areas including illustration, photography, design and photo illustration. He counts among his clients, Hertz Car Rental, Jiffy Lube, Yamaha, Paramount Pictures and Paper Moon.

Steve Vance and Matt Groening, creator of *The Simpsons* and the *Life in Hell* comic strip, have collaborated on many projects over the last decade, including greeting cards, posters, books and magazines. Their shared aesthetic is inspired by a lifelong diet of comic books, obscure movies and old jazz albums. As a child, Steve idolized the makers of popular culture. It makes him very happy to now be creating some of it himself.

Michael Conway grew up drawing what he saw in front of an RCA color TV in Houston, Texas, because "it was just too damned hot to play outside." At sixteen he picked up a Paper Moon card of Dave Willardson's Marilyn Monroe, and found his purpose in life. He studied Fine Art at Kansas City Art Institute and illustration at Otis/Parsons where he later taught. Today he is an art director in Los Angeles and doesn't spend enough time in front of the TV.

David Peters has lived and traveled extensively in Europe, the Middle East and Africa. His widely varied work experience includes stints as a stevedore, farm worker, deckhand in the Norwegian Merchant Marine, art teacher, professional photographer, animator and video producer. Since 1979 he has been a freelance illustrator specializing in collage. His musical clients include Ron Wood, Crosby Stills & Nash, Devo, and Weird Al Yankovic. Besides Paper Moon, his other clients include Diamond Toys, ABC and NBC TV, and CBS/Sony. David is a long-time collector of "stuff," primarily mid-20th-century pop culture novelty items, such as salt and pepper shakers, PEZ dispensers, dinosaurabilia, ray guns, snowdomes, toy banks, science fiction, space-related toys and other kitsch.

Greeting Card
Designers
Matt Groening and Steve Vance
Creative Director
Robert M. Fitch
Design Firm
Paper Moon Graphics, Inc., California

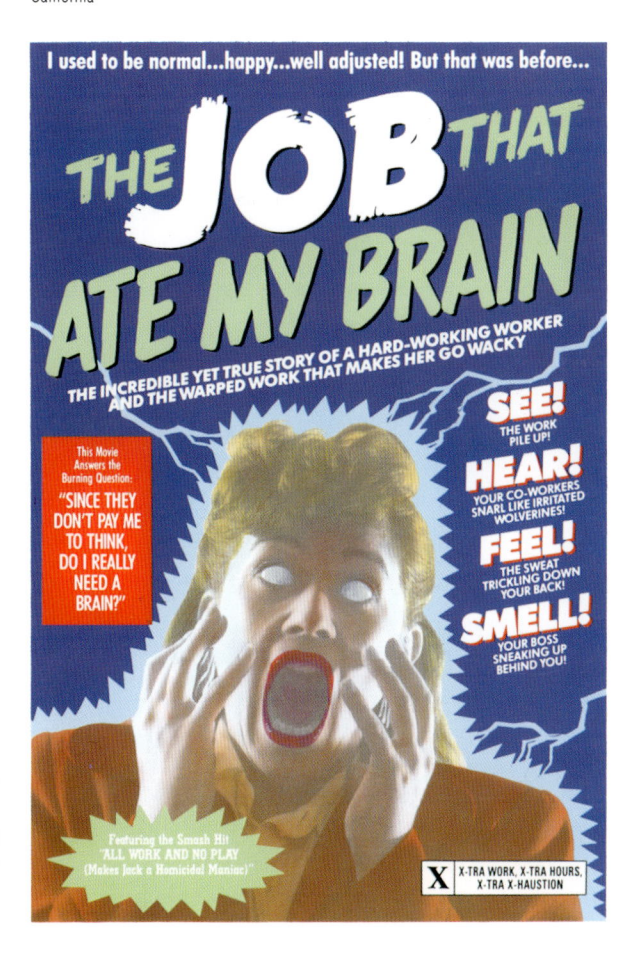

Retro Cadillac
Designer
Michael D. Conway
Creative Director
Robert M. Fitch
Design Firm
Paper Moon Graphics, Inc., California

61

In the same year that Elvis Presley had his first number one hit, Jim Ladwig began at Mercury Records in Chicago, working with the likes of Quincy Jones, Dinah Washington, Sarah Vaughn, and the Platters. At Mercury he met Don Kosterka who later suggested that they form a business to produce LP Jackets and AGI was founded in 1968. They developed the DIGIPAK for special edition packaging for use as a promotional tool and for sales at retail. The DIGIPAK is now a major retail option. So—the beat goes on, and the touch and feel are still pretty good too.

Al B. Sure
"Private Time…
And the Whole 9!"
Designer
Roger Gormans
Art Direction
Jeff Gold
Design Firm
Warner Brothers Records Inc., California
Photographer
Emil Warncke
© 1990 Warner Brothers Records Inc.

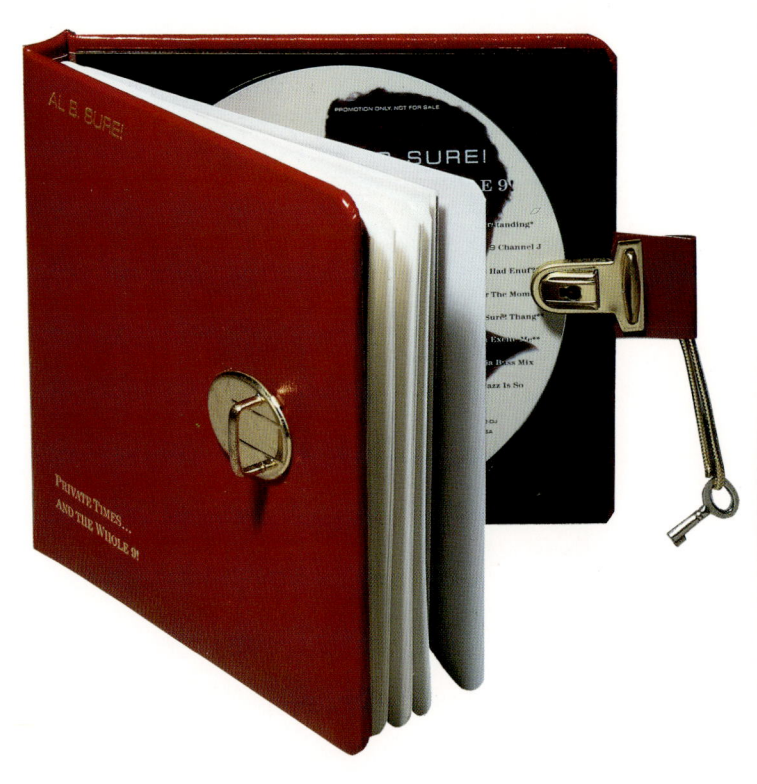

Pink Sunshine "Fuzzbox"
Art Direction
Samantha Hart
Design Firm
Geffen Records, California
© 1990 Geffen Records
Manufactured exclusively by
Warner Brothers Records

**Michelle Shocked
"On The Greener Side"**
Art Direction
Michael Bays
Design Firm
Polygram Records, New York
Photographer
Emil Warncke
© 1989 Polygram Songs Inc. (BMI)

63

WATERS DESIGN ASSOCIATES INC.

A native of North Carolina, John Waters received his BFA from the Virginia Commonwealth University, and later studied at MIT, New York University, and the School of Visual Arts in New York. He has received international recognition for his design including citations for excellence from the American Institute of Graphic Arts, *Communication Arts*, *Graphis Annual*, *International Design*, The Mead Annual Report Show, The New York Art Directors Club, and the American Center for Design.

Dreaming in Public
Designers
Dana Gonsalves and John Waters
Design Firm
Waters Design Associates, Inc., New York

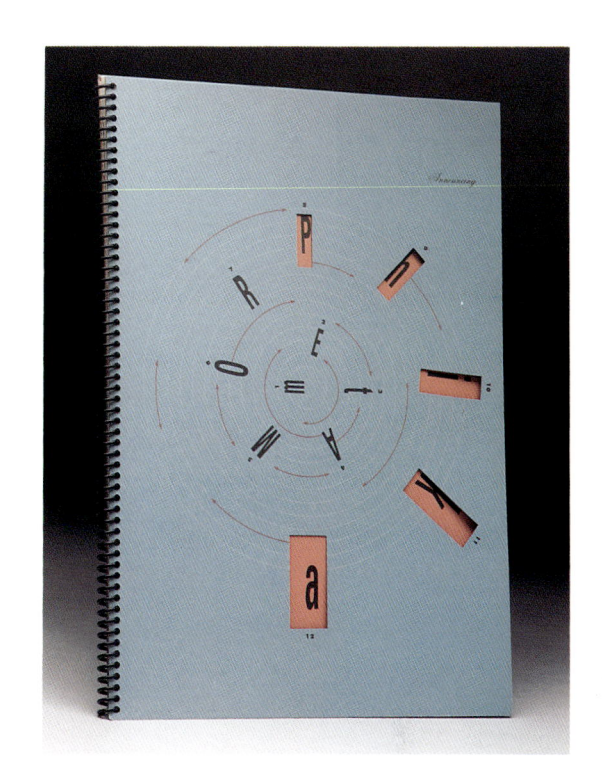

Curtis Tuscan Antique
and Tuscan Terra
Designer
Carol Bouyoucos
Design Firm
Waters Design Associates, Inc.,
New York

Metamorphika For Graphika
Designer
Carol Bouyoucos
Illustrators
Carol Bouyoucos and Dana Gonsalves
Design Firm
Waters Design Associates, Inc.,
New York

Graphika
Designers
Carol Bouyoucos and John Waters
Illustrator
Charlotte Knox
Design Firm
Waters Design Associates, Inc.,
New York
Photographers
Nola Lopez, Ken Merfeld,
Scott Morgan, Frank Okenfels
and Tim Simmons

65

MAKOTO SAITO

Dance Hall
Designer
Makoto Saito
Design Firm
Makoto Saito Design Office Inc.,
Tokyo
Photographer
Tsutomu Wakatsuki

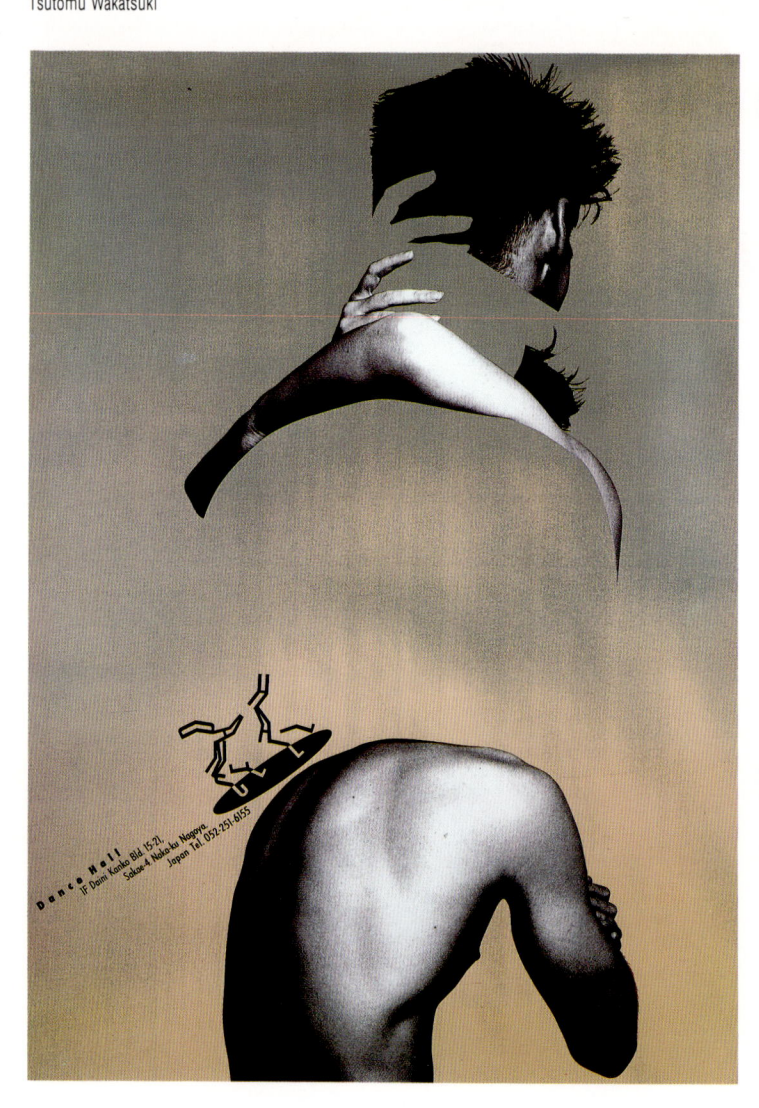

1986 Alpha Cubic
Designer
Makoto Saito
Design Firm
Makoto Saito Design Office Inc.,
Tokyo
Photographer
Eiichiro Sakata

1988 Alpha Cubic
Designer
Makoto Saito
Design Firm
Makoto Saito Design Office Inc.,
Tokyo
Photographer
Eiichiro Sakata

Kind Wear
Designer
Makoto Saito
Design Firm
Makoto Saito Design Office Inc., Tokyo

Tunnels No Teuchi
Designer
Makoto Saito
Design Firm
Makoto Saito Design Office Inc., Tokyo
Photographer
Eiichiro Sakata

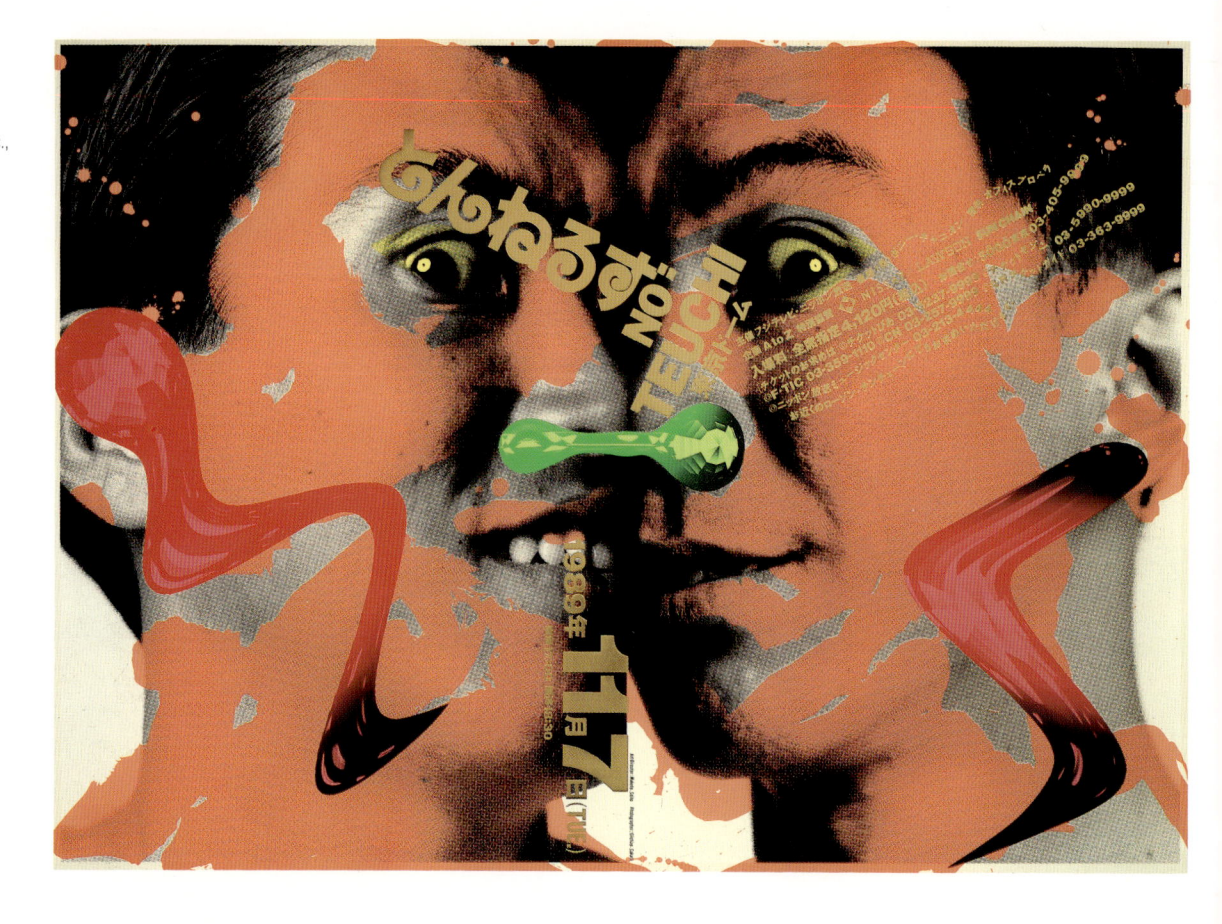

MAKOTO SAITO

0001 Alpha Cubic
Designer
Makoto Saito
Design Firm
Makoto Saito Design Office Inc.
Tokyo

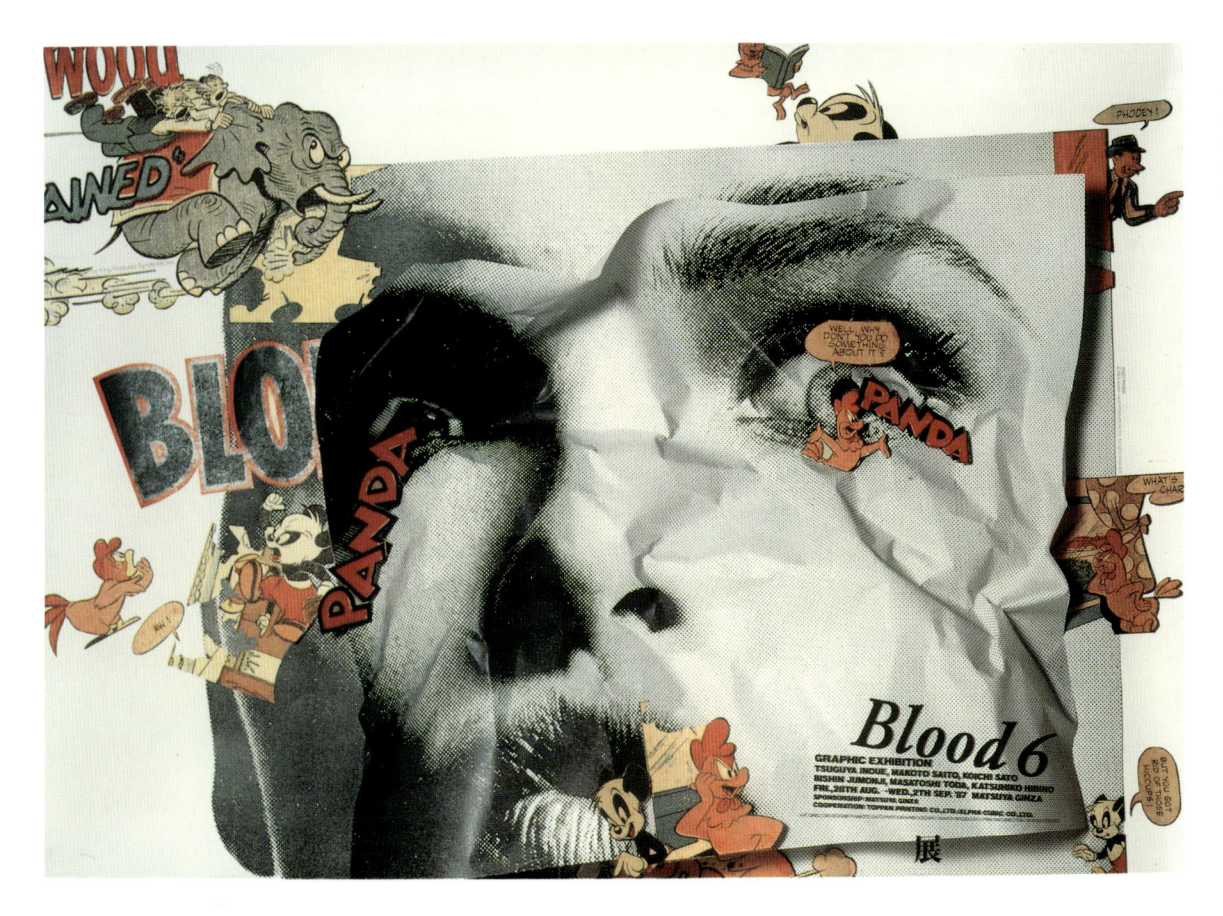

Blood 6
Designer
Makoto Saito
Design Firm
Makoto Saito Design Office Inc.,
Tokyo
Photographer
Eiichiro Sakata and Hiroshi Sato

Taiyo Printing Imagemirror
Designer
Makoto Saito
Design Firm
Makoto Saito Design Office Inc., Tokyo
Photographer
Tsutomu Wakatsuki

Garo
Designer
Makoto Saito
Design Firm
Makoto Saito Design Office Inc., Tokyo
Photographer
Hiroshi Yoda

MAKOTO SAITO

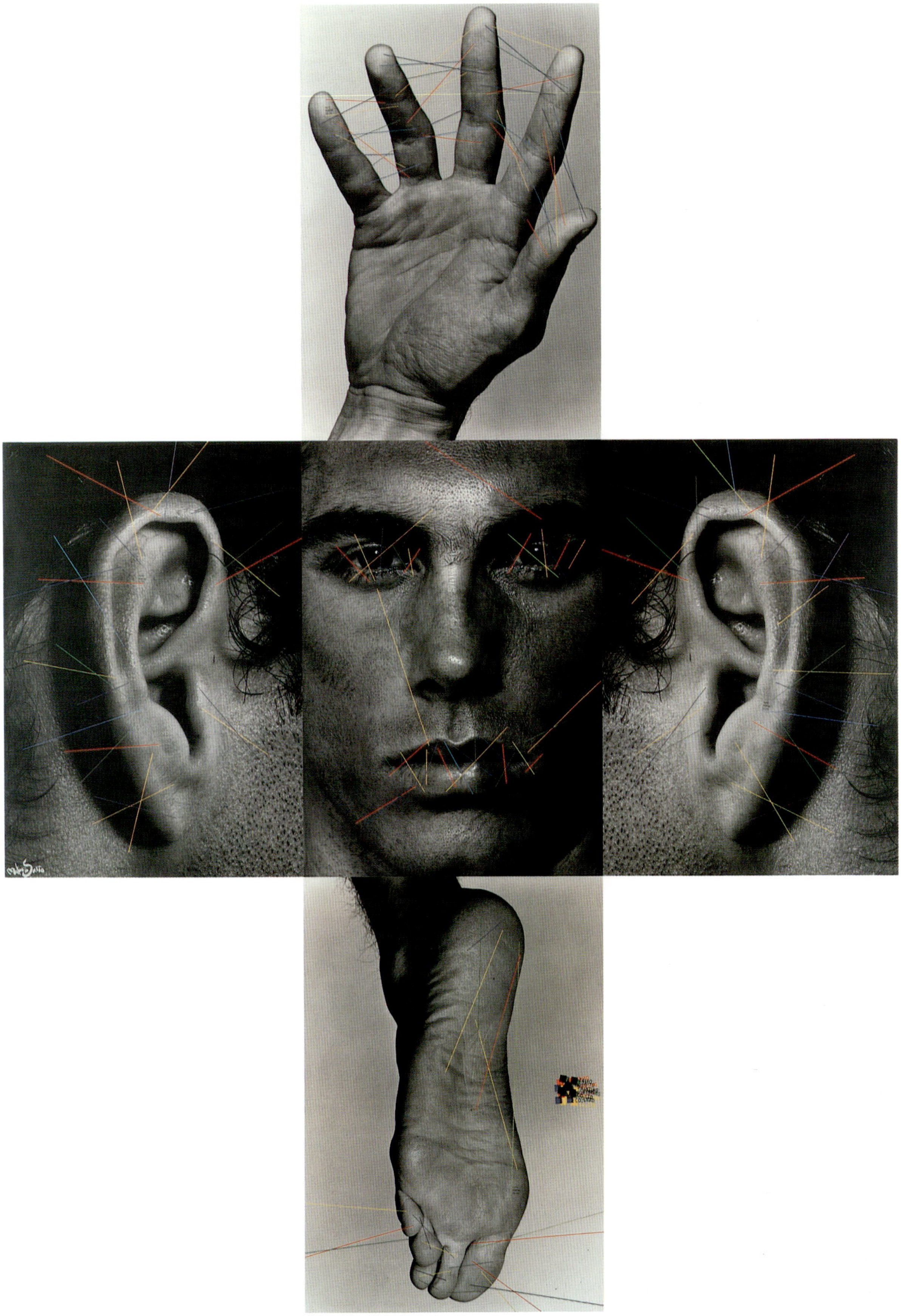

Taiyo Printing Imagemirror II
"The Cross"
Designer
Makoto Saito
Design Firm
Makoto Saito Design Office Inc.,
Tokyo
Photographer
Noboru Morikawa

CHRIS HARVEY

born under questionable circumstances, Chris Harvey was raised in the Texas desert by giant wasps. Early foraging skills yielded a steady diet of animated films, southern revival, and disposable food packaging. Retinal skills followed.

Currently continuing a series of esoteric devotional paintings, Chris urges everyone to get out and vote!

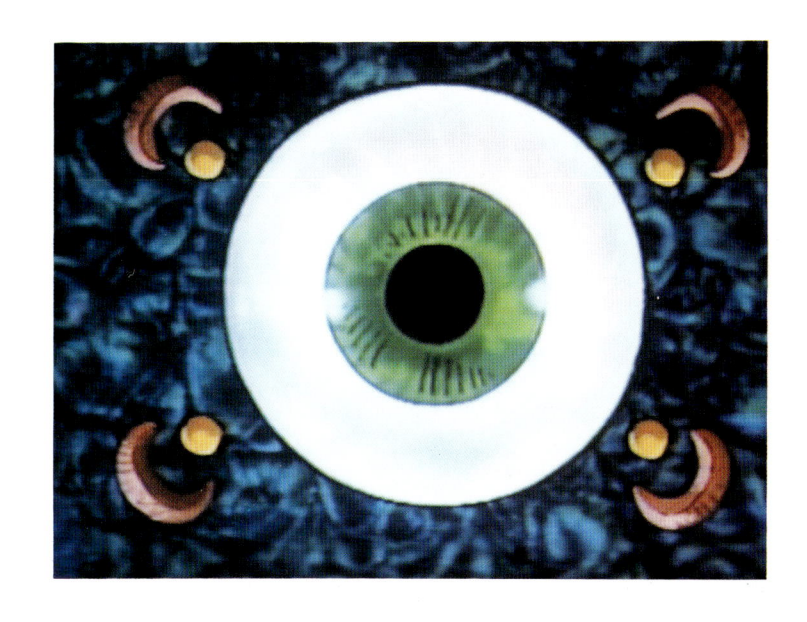

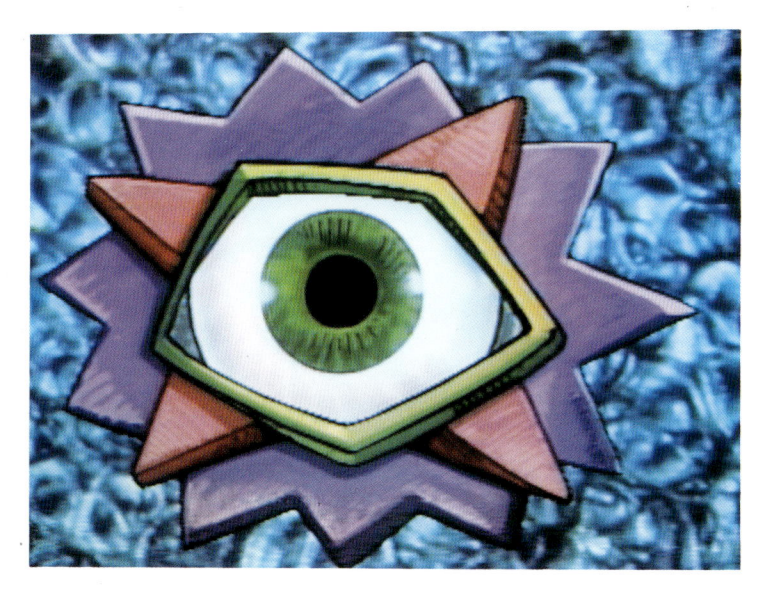

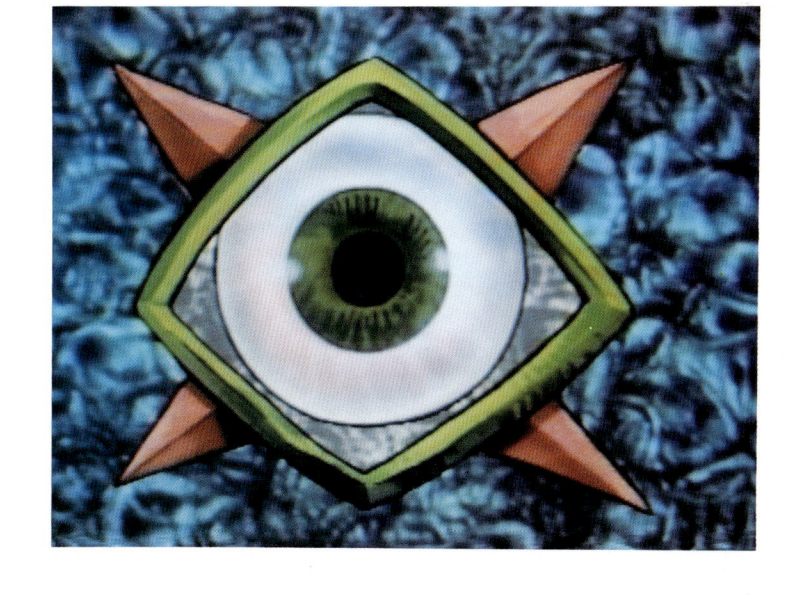

MTV Big Show (opener)
Designer
Chris Harvey
Art Director
Chris Harvey
Design Firm
Chris Harvey, New York

SIEBERT DESIGN

University of
Cincinnati College
Conservatory of Music
Recruiting Brochure

Designers
Lori Siebert and David Carroll

Design Firm
Siebert Design Associates, Inc.,
Ohio

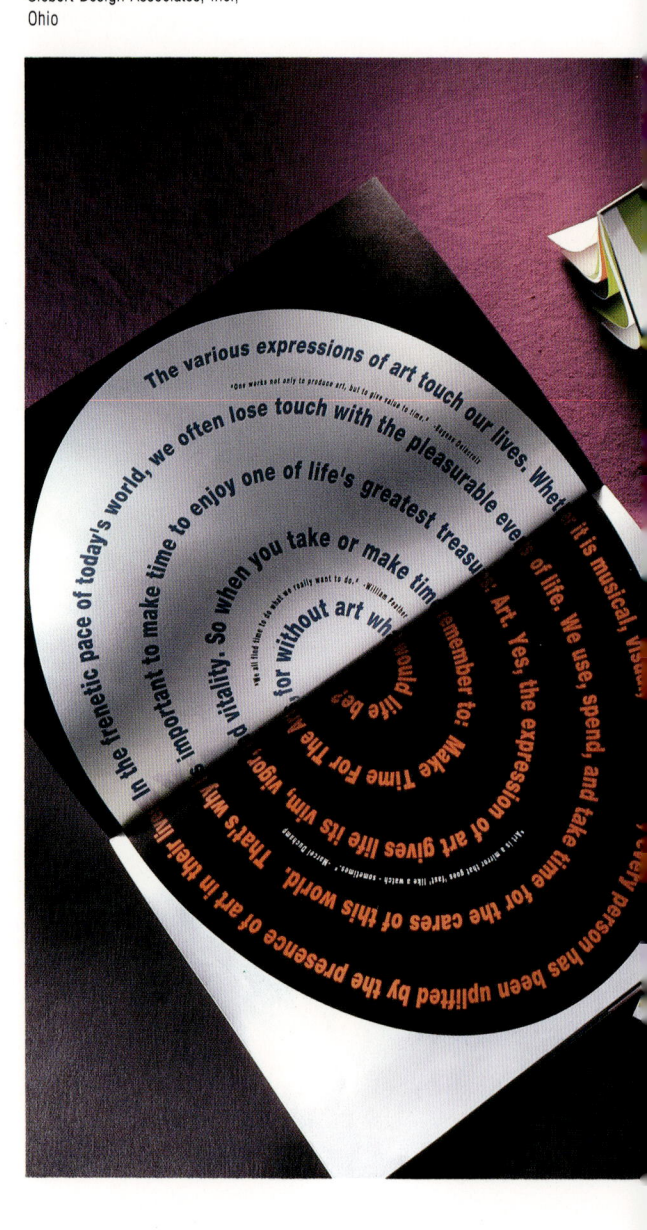

ori Siebert is president and Creative Director of Siebert Design Associates, Inc. a multifaceted design firm offering two dimensional and three dimensional graphic consultation to major corporations. She formed the company in May of 1987, just three years after graduating Summa cum laude from the University of Cincinnati's College of Design, Architecture, Art and Planning.

Printing by Design
Capabilities Book
Designer
Lori Siebert
Design Firm
Siebert Design Associates, Inc., Ohio
Photographer
Jeff Friedman

75

Frans Lieshout was born in Hoorn, The Netherlands. He began his career working as a hot metal typesetter at Stumpel, a printing shop. He has studied at the Graphic School of Amsterdam as well as the Rietveld Academy of Amsterdam. He has worked at Total Design and taught typography classes at Ecole Superieure d'Arts Graphiques in Paris, the Academy St. Joost at Breda, and the Academy of Modern Art in Rotterdam. Since 1992 he has been at work as a designer at Design Connection.

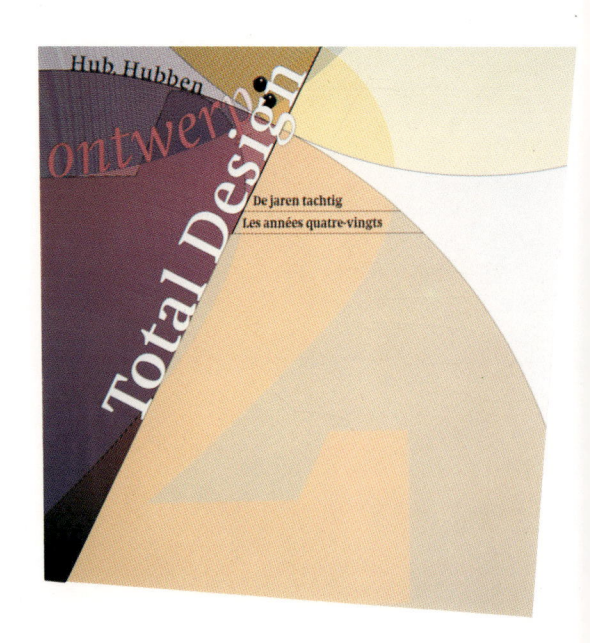

Corporate Book—
Total Design 2
Designer
Frans Lieshout
Design Firm
Total Design
Photographer
Sherry Kamp

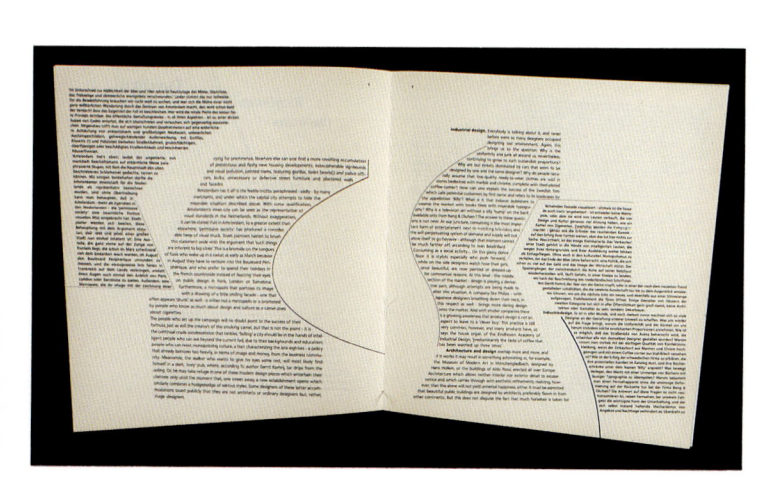

Poster About
the Nuclear Arms Race
Designer
Frans Lieshout
Design Firm
Frans Lieshout

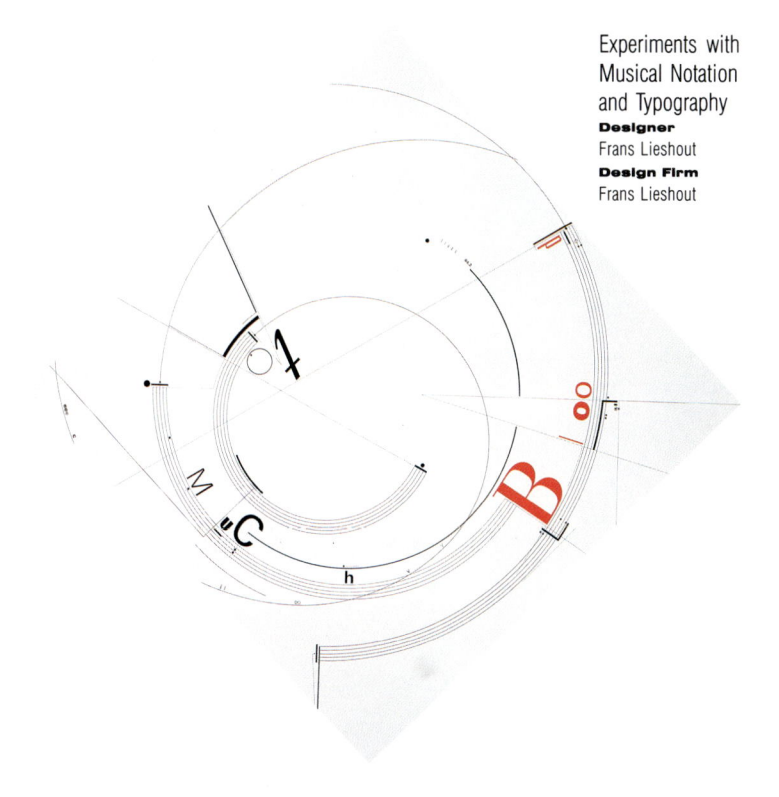

Experiments with
Musical Notation
and Typography
Designer
Frans Lieshout
Design Firm
Frans Lieshout

77

CHIP KIDD

Photo by Geoff Spear

Chip Kidd was born in Shillington, Pennsylvania in 1964. He is employed as Art Director and graphic designer at Alfred A. Knopf, a publisher in New York and an institution rife with traditions and the need to maintain them. Overheard: "Luckily for me, it has been Knopf's tradition since its inception in 1915, to provoke, to defy convention, to express often upsetting ideas, and to think about things in an unexpected fashion. It is these traditions that I mean to continue, to uphold."

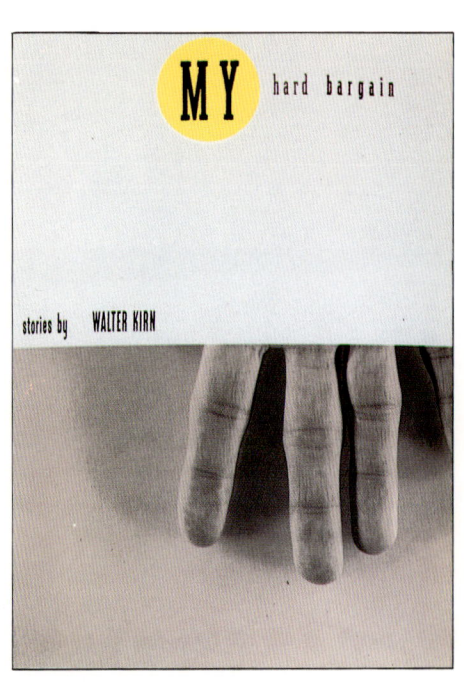

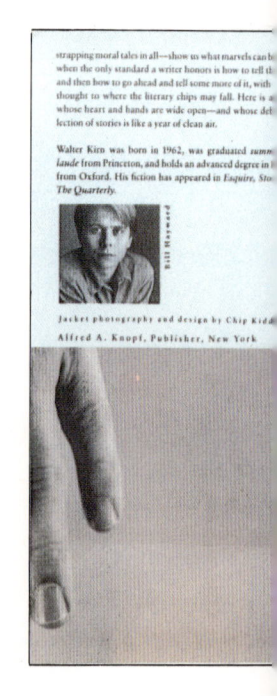

I HAD NEVER SEEN ANYONE ON FIRE BEFORE. CERTAINLY NOT MY FATHER.

MY hard bargain

stories by WALTER KIRN

strapping moral tales in all—show us what marvels can b
when the only standard a writer honors is how to tell th
and then how to go ahead and tell some more of it, with
thought to where the literary chips may fall. Here is a
whose heart and hands are wide open—and whose deb
fiction of stories is like a year of clean air.

Walter Kirn was born in 1962, was graduated summ
laude from Princeton, and holds an advanced degree in f
from Oxford. His fiction has appeared in Esquire, Sto
The Quarterly.

Jacket photography and design by Chip Kidd

Alfred A. Knopf, Publisher, New York

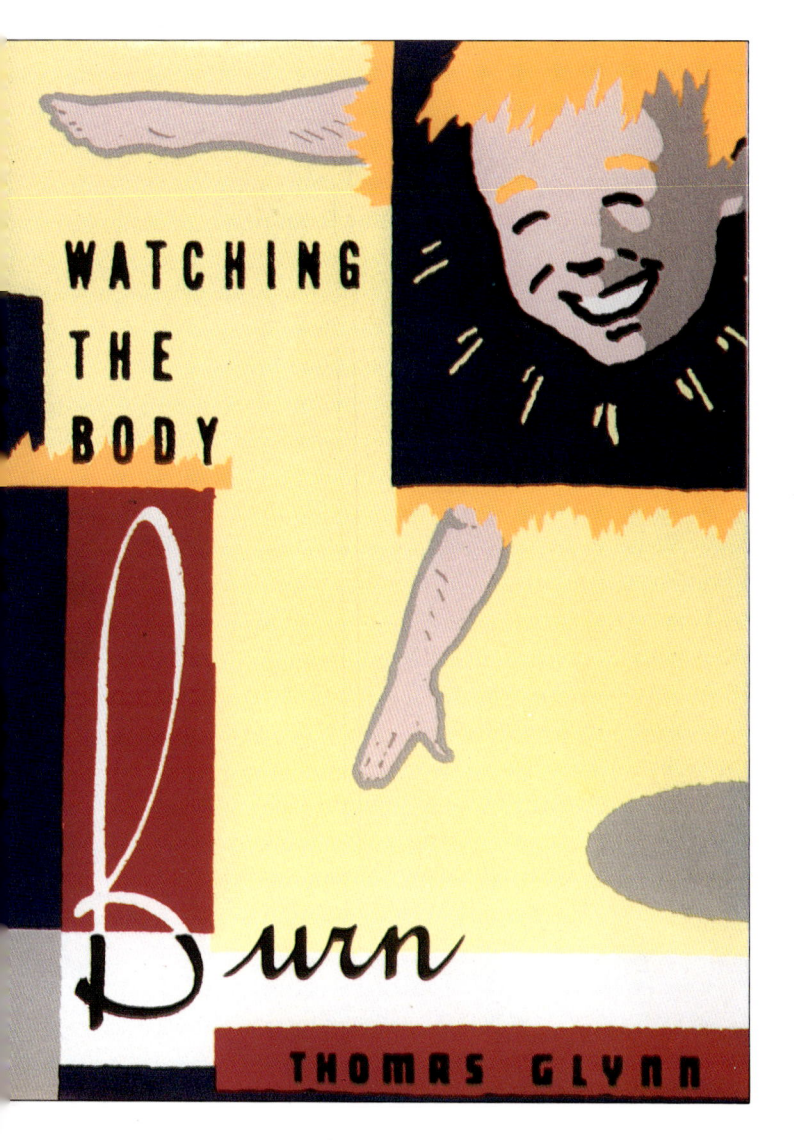

The American Replacement of Nature
by William Irwin Thompson
Designer
Barbara deWilde and Chip Kidd
Photographer
Barbara deWilde and Chip Kidd

Watching The Body Burn
by Thomas Glynn
Designer
Chip Kidd
Illustrator
Chip Kidd

My Hard Bargain
Stories by Walter Kirn
Designer
Chip Kidd
Art Director
Devine Carson
Photographer
Chip Kidd

79

MIKE SALISBURY

mike Salisbury's first real job was as Art Director of *Surfer Magazine* in 1962. He has since gone on to be Associate Art Director for *Playboy*, Art Director for *West Magazine*, and a freelance photographer for *Vogue*, *Esquire*, *Time-Life*, and *Look* magazines. He was also Creative Director for UA Records and received a Grammy nomination for album cover design. In 1974–75 as Art Director of *Rolling Stone* he redesigned the magazine. In 1980–81 as Director of Creative Services at Foote Cone and Belding he created the Levis 501 brand.

Gotcha—Catalog
"Hard Line '90"

Design Firm
Mike Salisbury Communications Inc.,
California
Photographer
Mike Funk

Gotcha—Catalog "Spring '91"
Designer
Mike Salisbury
Design Firm
Mike Salisbury Communications Inc.,
California
Photographer
Mike Funk

81

Gotcha—Catalog "Spring '90"
"More Core Journal"
Designer
Mike Salisbury
Design Firm
Mike Salisbury Communications Inc.,
California
Photographer
Mike Salisbury

MIKE SALISBURY

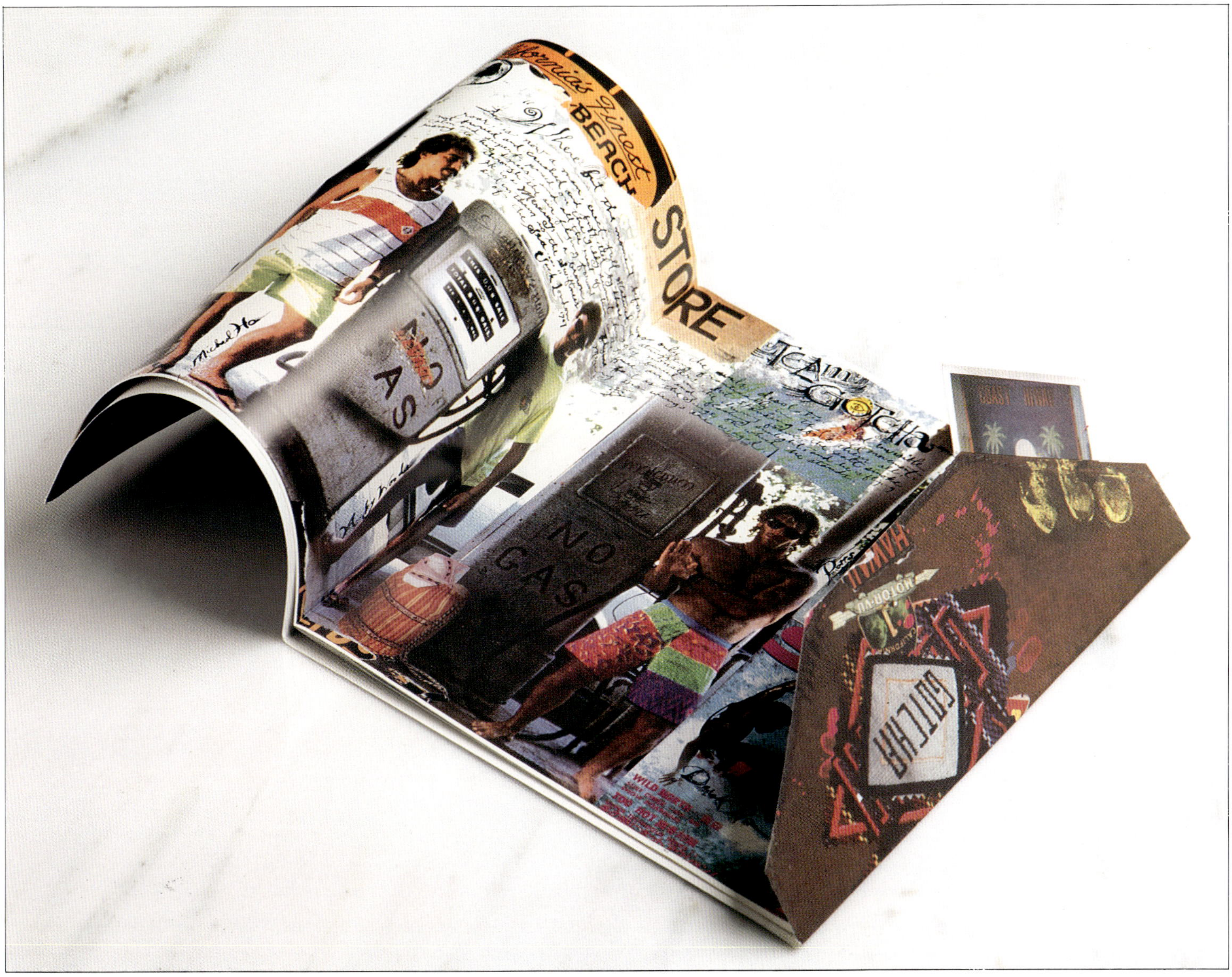
BEACH
STORE
NO GAS

Halley's Comet Poster
Designer
Edwin Torres
Design Firm
Edwin Torres, New York

ICJOW: In explanation of collaboration."

esJamesJma himhe dance with his eyes by hands to his A to Z him from in to his mades of antique cards, imagily that! Jolly he, Let me Let it, I say. He let it me see it I play a sayword game. Say he, Let's do it the different! He say I say. That's all is that one have fun tiny we. Sit in your hand. Open. Open. Intuitive. In Two It Is. The pattern reverse...?...Blackwhite his each letter a tri-tone two blacks and a grey dancing in miniature dancily versily KICJOW!...makes a WOJCIK...Who is it that gets that? People do it. Get laughily let its, get listen to touch say it to thinkits.

Etthhe pletecomcomplete labetphabetla...all 26...52?ha ha words into more become photovisual become lingualvisual becomes fun becomes more work for James.

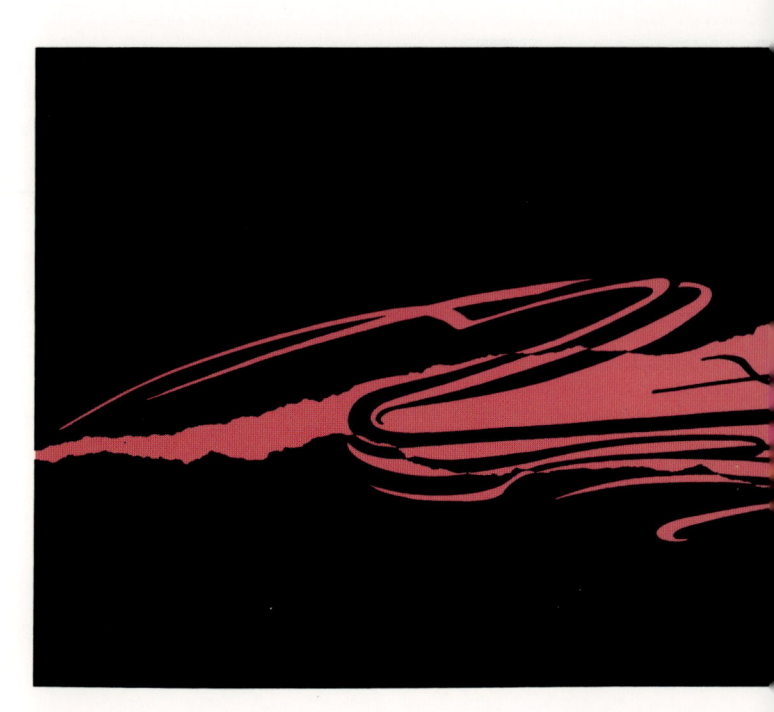

Promotion Piece for Wojcik
Designer
Edwin Torres
Photographer
James Wojcik
© 1991 James Wojcik

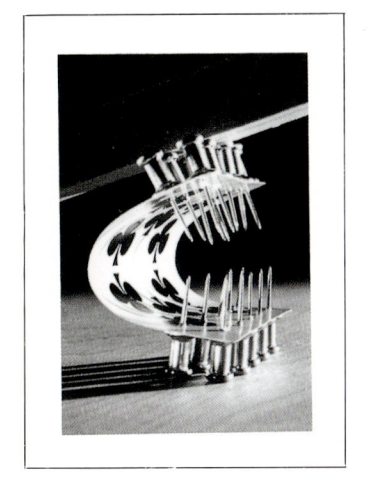

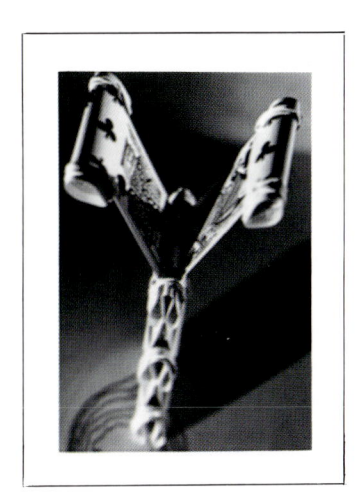

California-born New York designer and illustrator Mike Quon was originally scheduled to be a dentist. A graduate of UCLA, he studied in a general design and advertising program and continued his education at the Art Center College of Design. There he realized his talent and personality was to take him into different areas: Mike Quon the designer and Mike Quon the illustrator. He calls himself a design generalist—and he and his staff move comfortably from logo design, to posters, brochures, systems, corporate literature, advertising illustration, signage, exhibit and even product design. He believes that you can serve a client and still be daring and attention getting. Mike loves to travel, and he has an ongoing ten year project in which he has photographed over a thousand people with his "Q" logo.

45 Year-Old Chinese Man
Designer
Mike Quon
Design Firm
Mike Quon Design Office

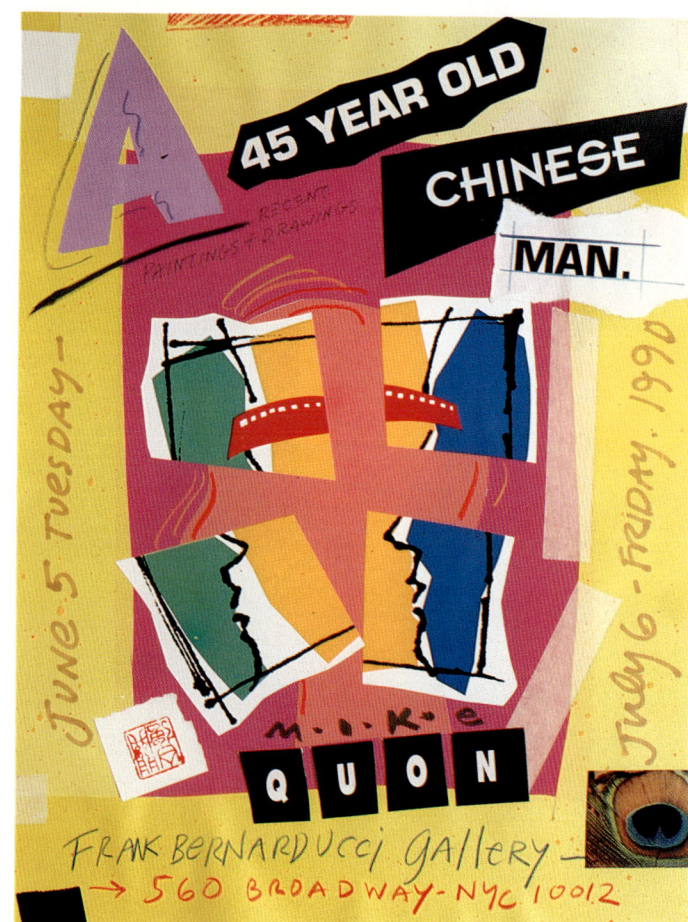

Futuristic Mockery
Designer
Mike Quon
Design Firm
Mike Quon Design Office

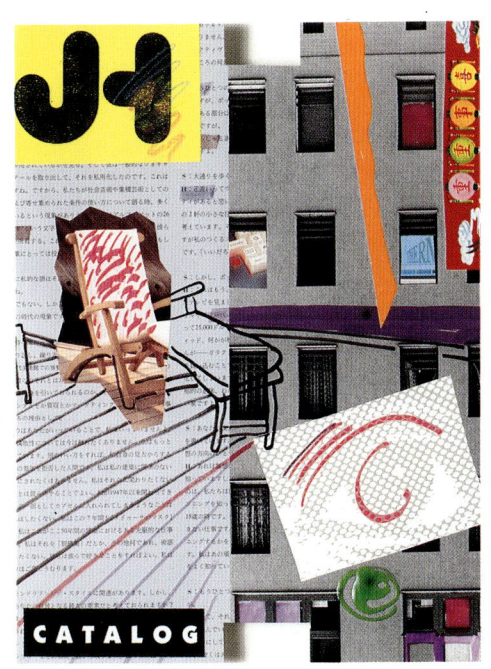

JH Catalog
Designer
Mike Quon
Design Firm
Mike Quon Design Office

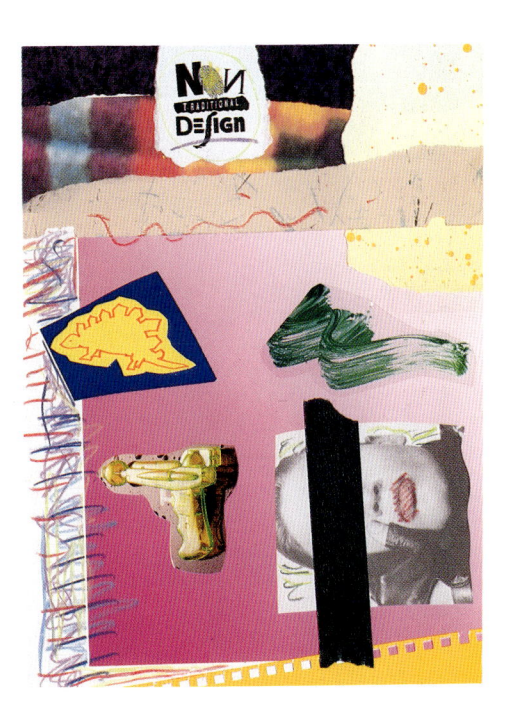

Non-Traditional Design
Designer
Mike Quon
Design Firm
Mike Quon Design Office

"By combining my Asian roots with my western upbringing I'm trying to create a new point of view. I'm excited about the role of the designer in today's society. I can see the boundary between fine art and advertising art blurring. With my own career I try to have as much fun as I can. I like to see it as a work in progress and try to use a lot of color and energy to help entertain. It is also great to bring contrast and a mix of styles— these have always been favorite themes."

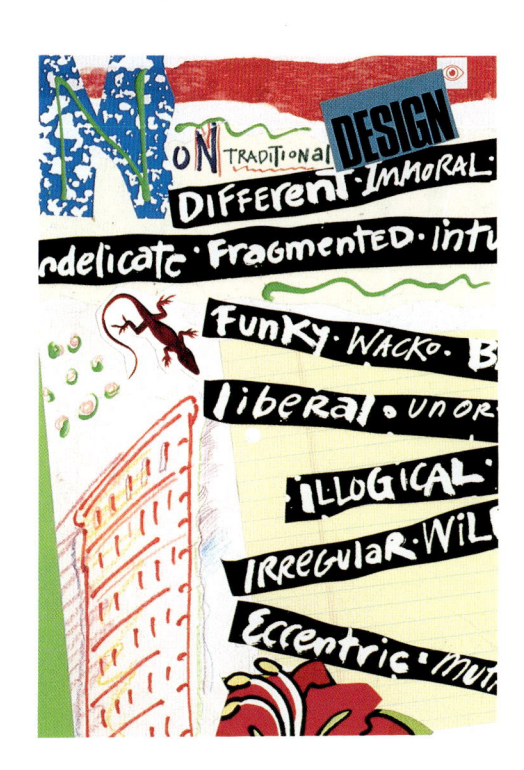

"Work has got to be fun!"

African Man
Designer
Mike Quon
Design Firm
Mike Quon Design Office

Non-Traditional Design
Designer
Mike Quon
Design Firm
Mike Quon Design Office

87

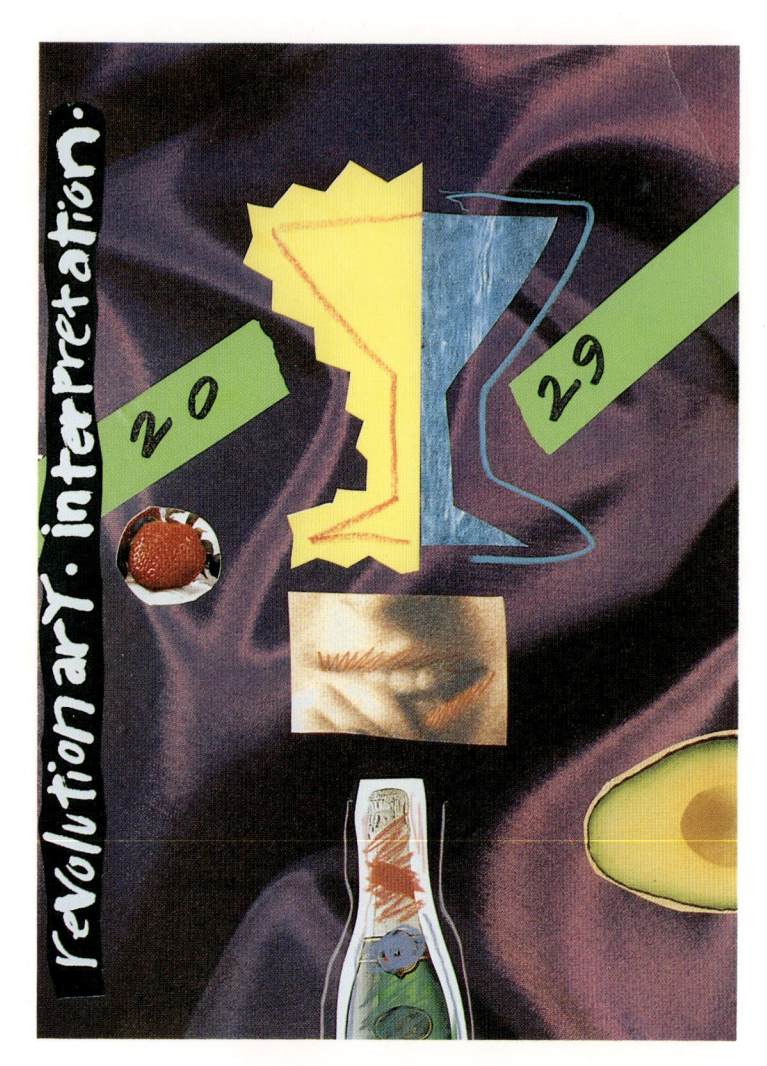

MIKE QUON

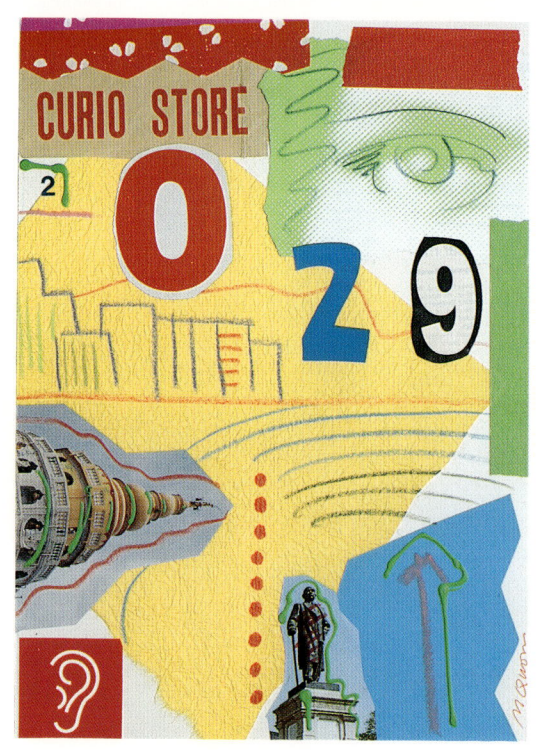

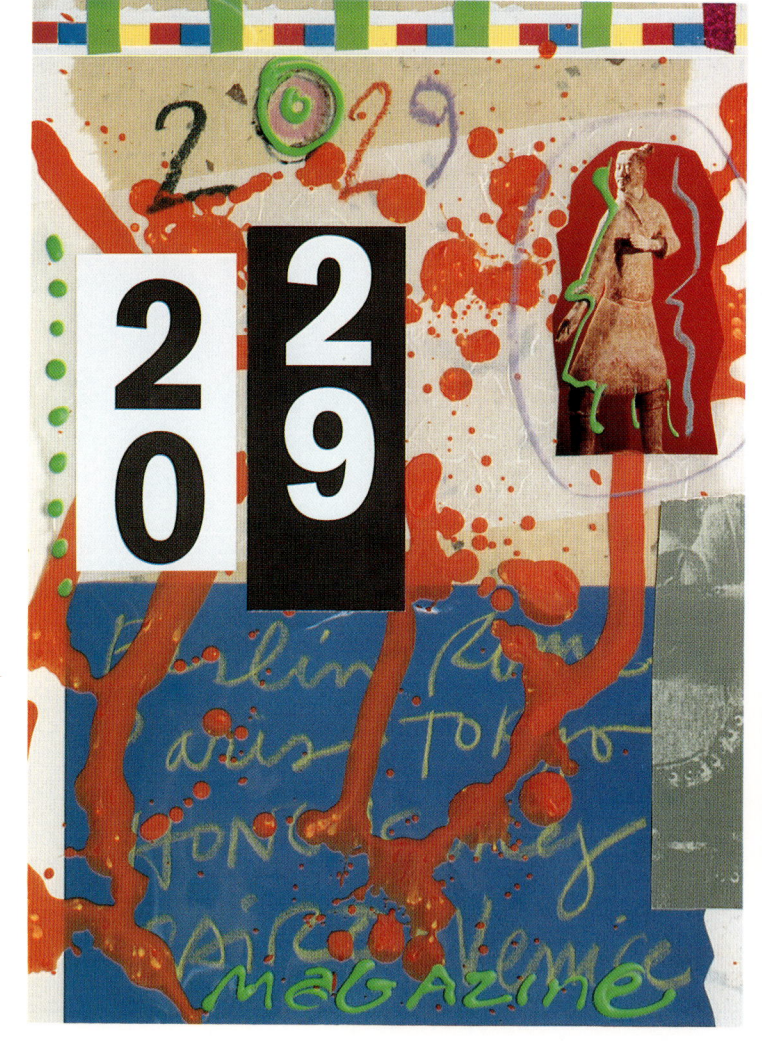

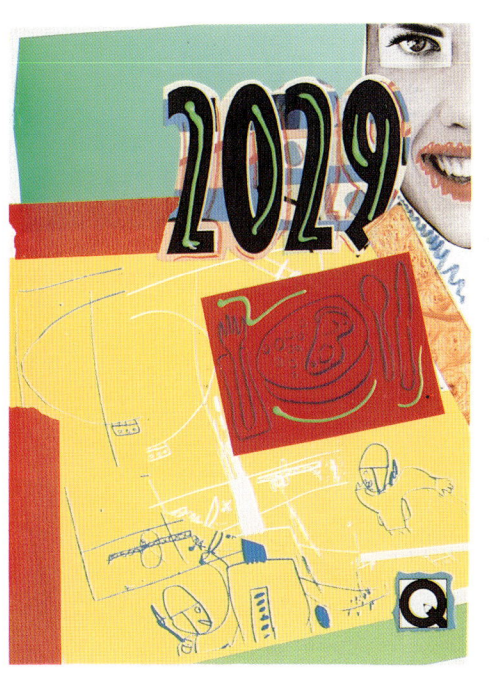

2029 Magazin
Designer
Mike Quon
Design Firm
Mike Quon Design Office

MICHAEL PETERS LTD.

Tsaritsa Vodka
Designer
Glenn Tutssel
Design Firm
Michael Peters Ltd., England

Ross Cordless Headphones
Designer
Karen Welman
Design Firm
Michael Peters Ltd., England

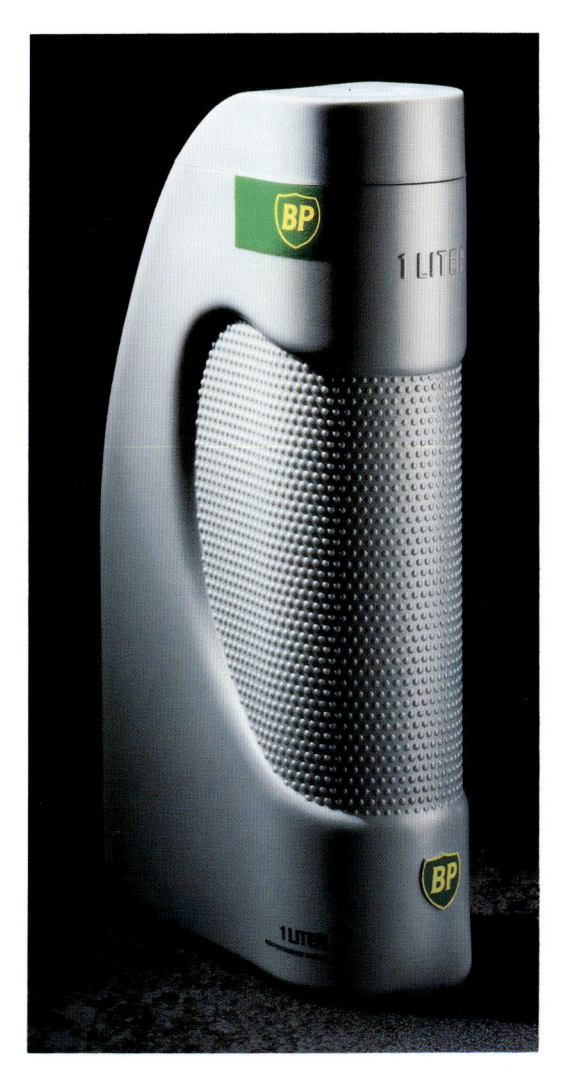

BP Oil Can
Designer
Garrick Hamm
Design Firm
Michael Peters Ltd., England

ASDA Tissues
Designer
David Pike
Design Firm
Michael Peters Ltd., England

Bathhouse Theater:
Shakespeare's MacBeth
Designer
Art Chantry
Design Firm
Art Chantry Design, Washington

Give Peace A Dance 1986
Designer
Art Chantry
Design Firm
Art Chantry Design, Washington

A rt Director of Seattle's *The Rocket* magazine and author of the book *INSTANT LITTER, concert Posters From Seattle Punk Culture*, Art Chantry has received recognition in fields ranging from typographic design to illustration. He has written extensively on design issues and has lectured at numerous other institutions such as ArtCenter, CalArts, Kent State University as well as others.

Give Peace A Dance 1987
Designer
Art Chantry
Design Firm
Art Chantry Design, Washington

New City Theater
Season Poster 1987
Designer
Art Chantry
Design Firm
Art Chantry Design, Washington

93

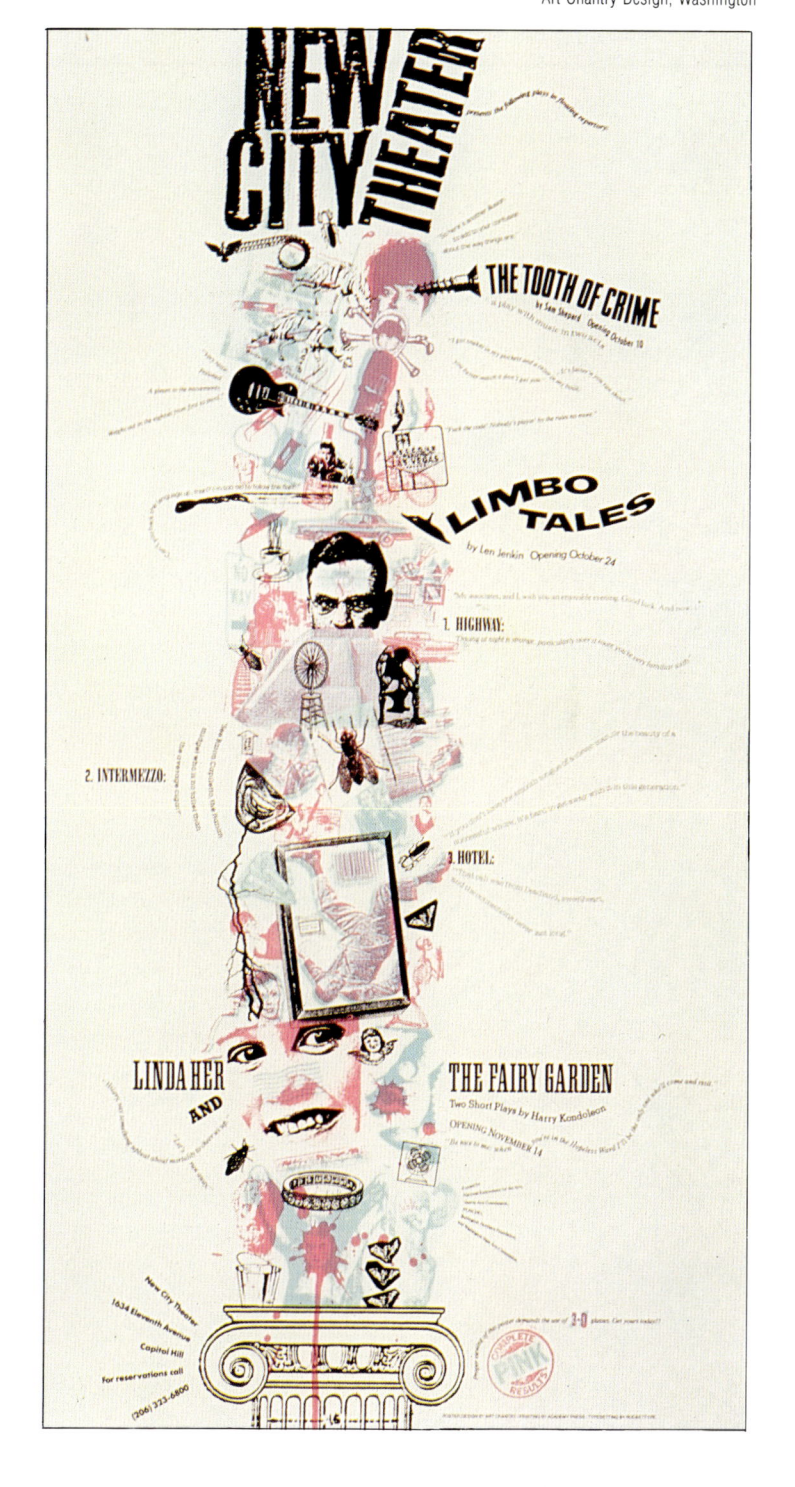

MILTON GLASER

Milton Glaser was a co-founder and president of Push Pin Studios until 1974, and co-founder, president, and creative director of *New York Magazine* until 1976. He has been president of Milton Glaser, Inc. since 1974. He is personally responsible for the design and illustration of over 300 posters for clients in the areas of publishing, music, theater, film, institutional and civic enterprise, as well as those for commercial and products services. In 1975 he had a one man show at the Museum of Modern Art in New York. A teacher and member of the board of directors at School of Visual Arts, he is also a trustee at Cooper Union.

Hidden Music
Designer
Milton Glaser
Design Firm
Milton Glaser, Inc., New York

ARMY TRAINER MAGAZINE

Army Trainer Magazine
Designer
Greg Willis
Photographer
Greg Willis

"*The Army is becoming increasingly conscious that design is an effective means of communication. A key element of marketing design is the effectiveness of the concept. A designer can take many directions to develop a concept. I prefer to use traditional components—typography, visuals and photography—to create non-traditional effects. I incorporate them into an extreme format in which they suggest some type of specific feel, something that will pull the viewer in instantly. Then, I incorporate additional plays on that direction, which the viewer perceives after his or her attention has been captured. I do this by varying size, shape, repetition and placement. Design should be functional. A spectacular appearance is a by-product of creativity.*"

BLACKDOG DESIGN

In 1986 Mark Fox founded Blackdog in San Francisco. In 1992 one of his political posters, "Kinder Gentler Carpet Bombing," was accepted into the permanent graphic design collection of the Library of Congress.

The Northern California Printbook
Designer
Mark Fox
Illustrator
Mark Fox
Design Firm
Blackdog, California

End
Designer
Mark Fox
Illustrator
Mark Fox
Design Firm
Blackdog, California
© *Mark Fox/Blackdog 1987*

"*Concept in design is a fine thing, but not if it's at the expense of emotion. Of all the arts, music impresses me most for its ability to evoke an emotional response. My work is about moving people to feel, think, or act.*"

Marianne Campbell
Designer
Mark Fox
Illustrator
Mark Fox
Design Firm
Blackdog, California

CRANBROOK ACADEMY OF ART

Katherine McCoy is CoChairman of the Department of Design at Cranbrook Academy of Art and partner of McCoy & McCoy Associates. Her work has been published and exhibited widely, including *Graphic Design in America: A Visual Language History* by the Walker Art Center, *L'image des Mots* at the Centre Pompidou Centre de Creation Industrielle, the Cooper Hewitt Museum of Design, and the American Institute of Graphic Arts. She has just co-authored and designed *Cranbrook Design: The New Discourse*, a book published by Rizzoli International.

Cranbrook Design Poster
Designer
Katherine McCoy
Printer
Signet
Design Firm
McCoy & McCoy, Michigan

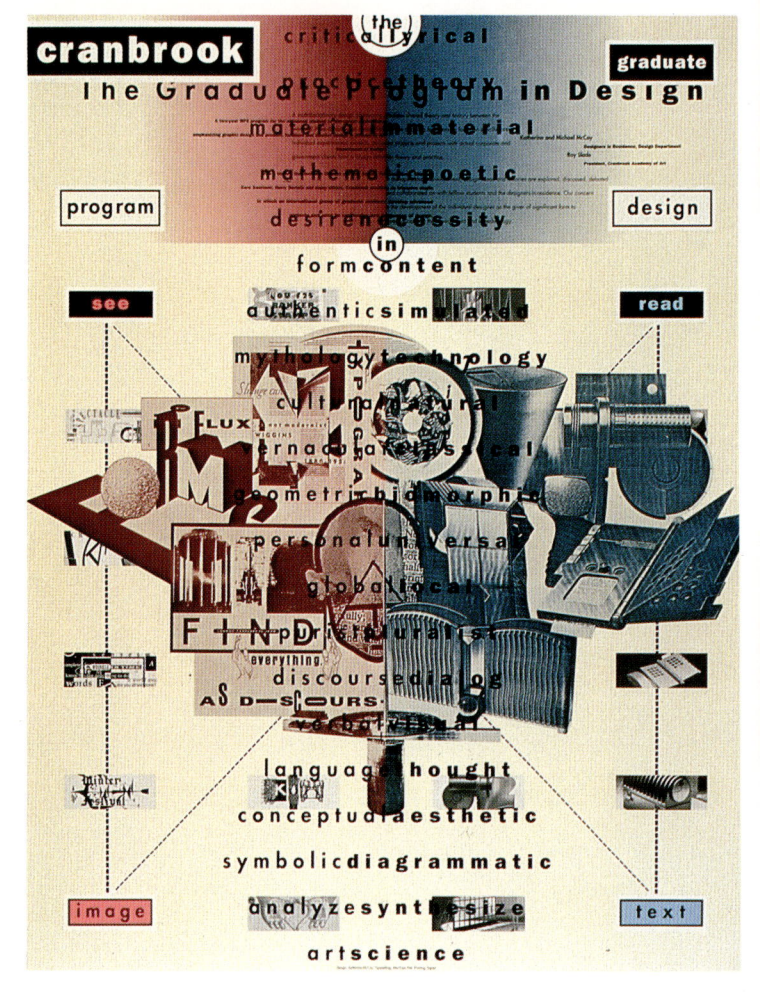

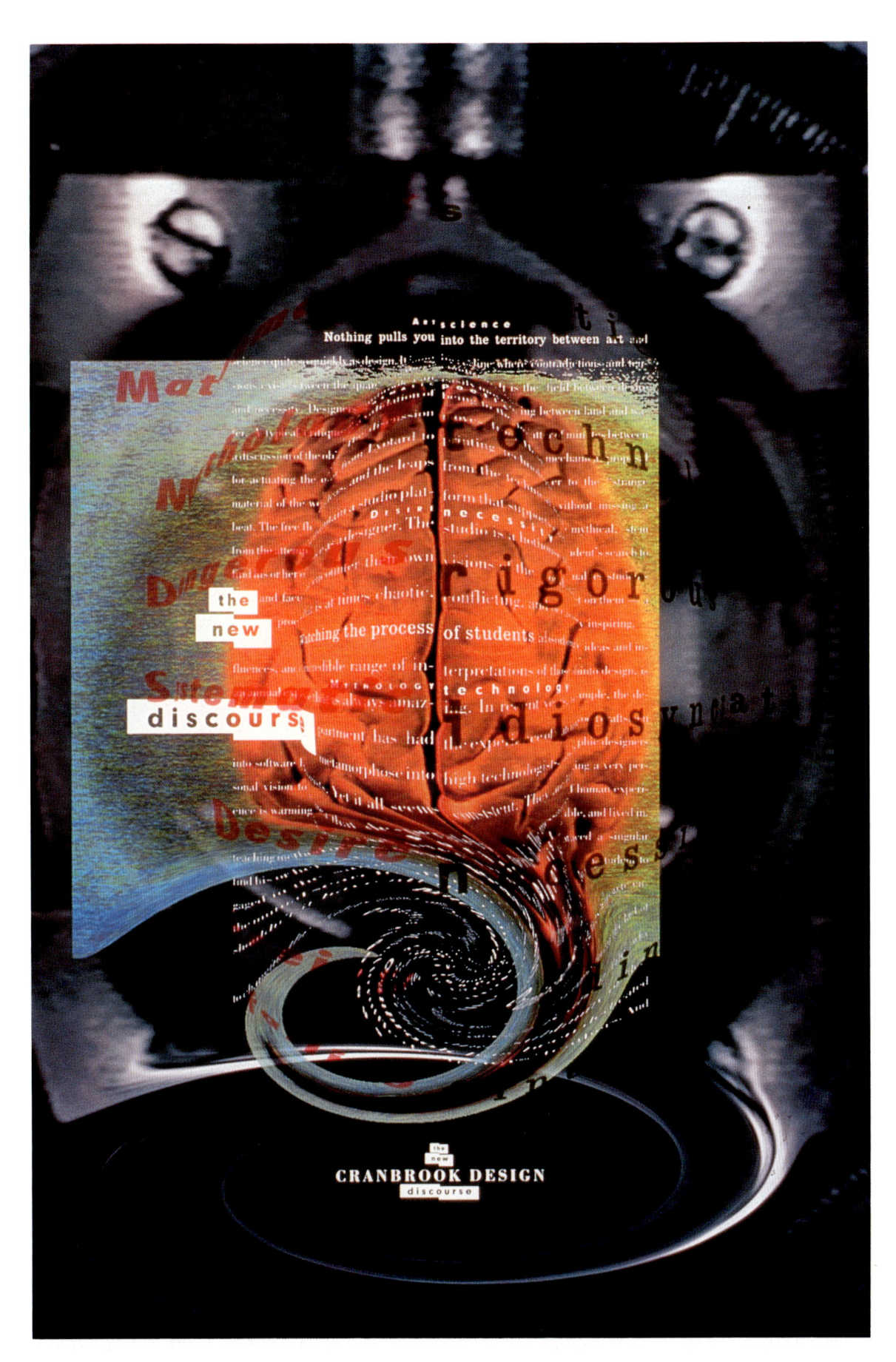

New Discourse Poster
Designer
P. Scott Makela
Printer
Typocraft
Design Firm
Cranbrook Academy of Art, Michigan

Red Square Signage
Designers
Tibor Kalman and Marlene McCarty
Design Firm
M & Co., New York
Photographer
Alexander Brebner

Naked Poster
Designers
Tibor Kalman and Douglas Riccardi
Monkey Painting
Paula Wright
Band
Chris Callis
Design Firm
M & Co., New York

Photo: Chris Callis

Born in Budapest in 1949, Tibor Kalman emigrated at age seven to Poughkeepsie, N.Y. By the age of sixteen he had his first real job as a shoe salesman laboring to stuff hundreds of feet into shoes three sizes too small. It was his first real contact with design problems. At New York University he studied journalism and failed art history. He later went on to become the Design Director for Barnes and Noble and in 1979 founded M&CO., a multi-disciplinary design firm that tries to reinvent the wheel for clients ranging from Knoll International to Talking Heads.

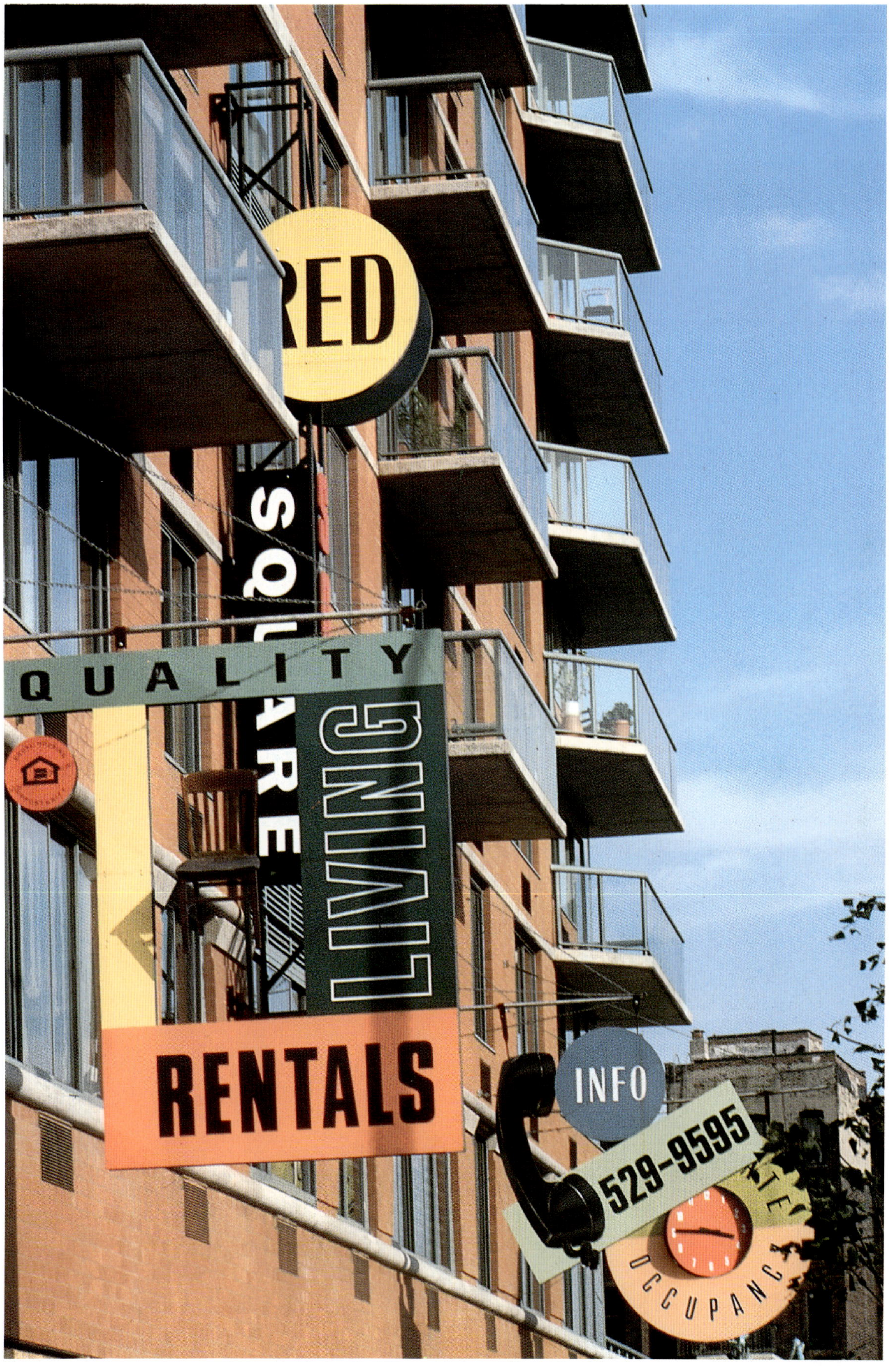
RED
QUALITY
LIVING
RENTALS
INFO
529-9595
OCCUPANC

"*We have an individual look that is ours alone and no other publication comes close by comparison. Quality, variety and style are what sets us apart from all the others.*"

German born Peter Forsten has been a dancer, gardener, model, actor, photographer's agent and is now a magazine publisher. Internationally unique, *2029 Magazin* is Forsten's "child." The publication focuses on a new and different theme with each issue. It is created from an artistic point of view with a strong emphasis on design. In each copy talented photographers, illustrators, writers, artists and designers are brought together. *2029 Magazin* represents the known, as well as the unknown from around the world.

2029 Magazin #6
"Architecture & Design"
Designers
Roy Nher, Christof Rabanus

2029 Magazin #7 "Motion"
Design Firm
Take Studio, Hamburg
Photographer
Take Studio, Hamburg

ANTHONY MA

Book of Idiots 2
Designer
Anthony Ma
Artists
Gary Leib and Doug Allen
Design Firm
A. Ma Design, Illinois

Life is Bliss
Designer
Anthony Ma
Design Firm
A. Ma Design, Illinois

Ten in One Gallery
Designer
Anthony Ma
Design Firm
A. Ma Design, Illinois

ANTHONY MA

109

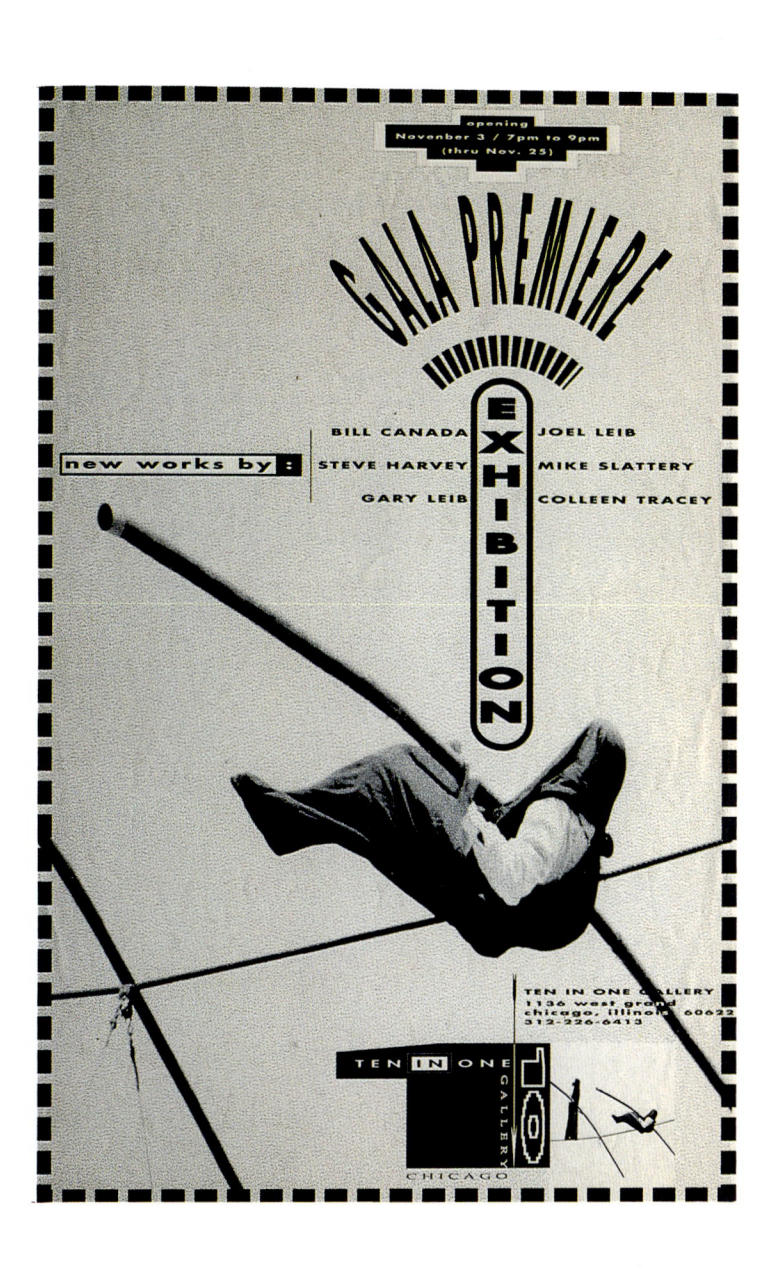

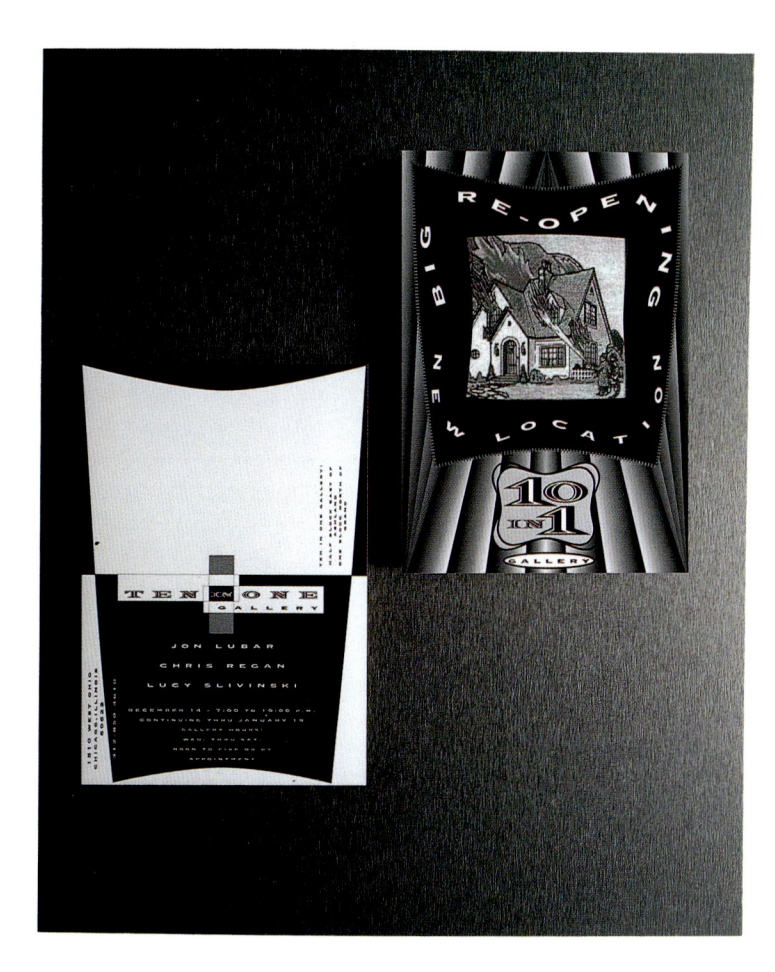

The "Faith"
Self Promotion Book
Designer
Paul Sych
Design Firm
Faith, Canada

Paul's specialization at the Ontario College of Art in Toronto was in communications and design. Because of his interest in jazz he was concurrently enrolled in the Jazz Studies Program at York University. As a senior Art Director at Reactor he began to explore and successfully complete assignments requiring significant typographic design input for a number of large corporations.

"*My belief is that, to get ahead you have to make a little noise. Noise whose frequencies are outside of the normal wavelengths. That noise might sound cacophonous to some—much like John Coltrane did—but so be it.*"

Promotional Cards
Designer
Paul Sych
Design Firm
Faith, Canada

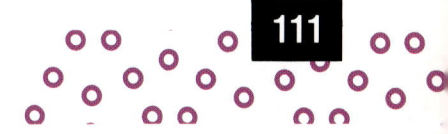

Promotional
Post Card Series For
Fontshop International
Designer
Paul Sych
Design Firm
Faith, Canada

"So & So"
Designer
Paul Sych
Design Firm
Faith, Canada

F A I T H

we've got to get so and so

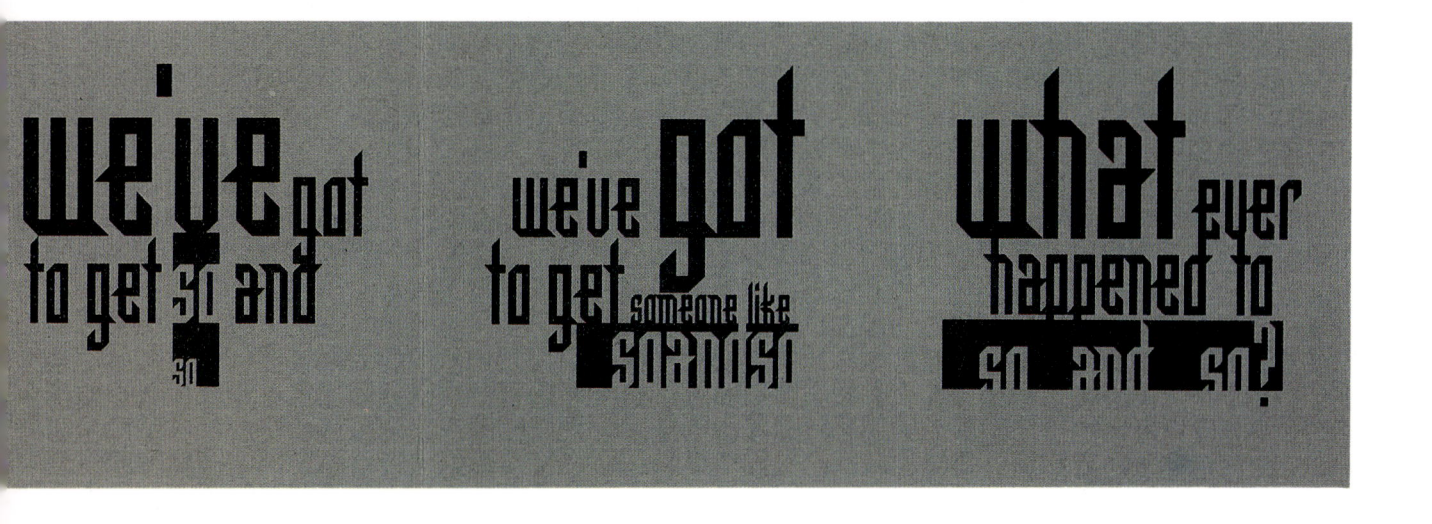

we've got to get someone like spanish

whatever happened to so and so?

TV Intro for
"The New Music"
Designer
Paul Sych
Typographer
Paul Sych
Art Director
Robin Len
Design Firm
Faith, Canada

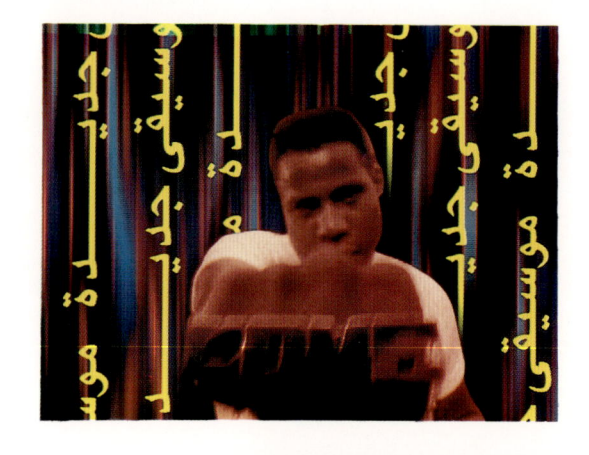

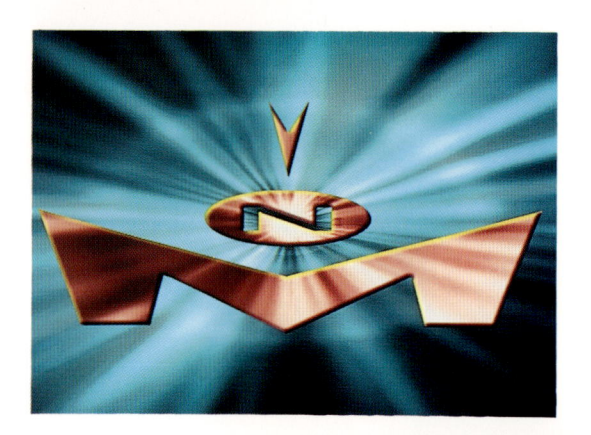

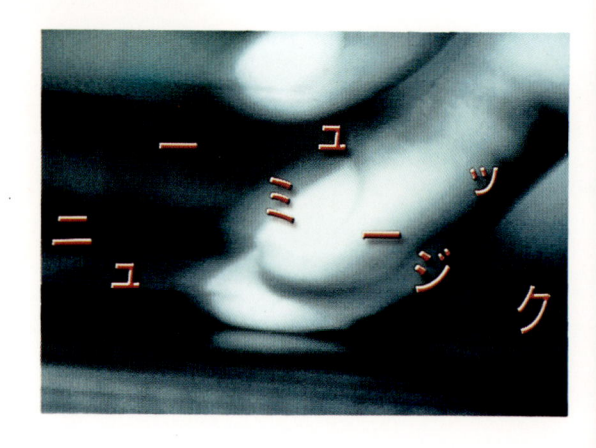

F A I T H

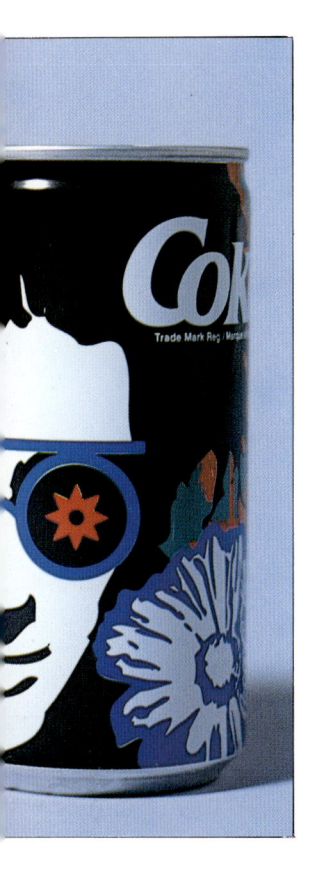

Coca-Cola Can Designs
Designer
Paul Sych
Typographer
Paul Sych
Art Director
Steve Blair

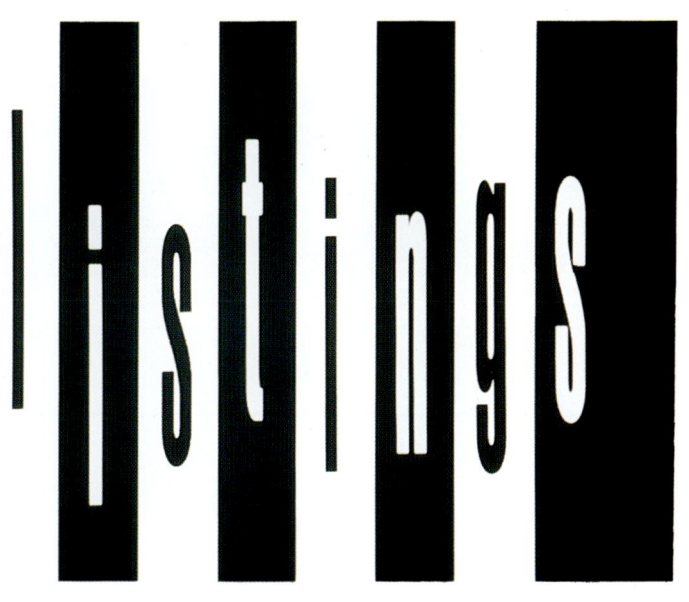

listings

TV Intro For "Much Music"
Designer
Paul Sych
Creative Director
Paul Sych
Art Director
Robin Len
Design Firm
Faith, Canada

115

Harry Metzler De Luxe
1991 Calendar
Designer
Harry Metzler
Design Firm
Harry Metzler Artdesign,
Schwartzenberg, Austria

Harry Metzler De Luxe
1990 Calendar
Designer
Harry Metzler
Design Firm
Harry Metzler Artdesign,
Schwartzenberg, Austria

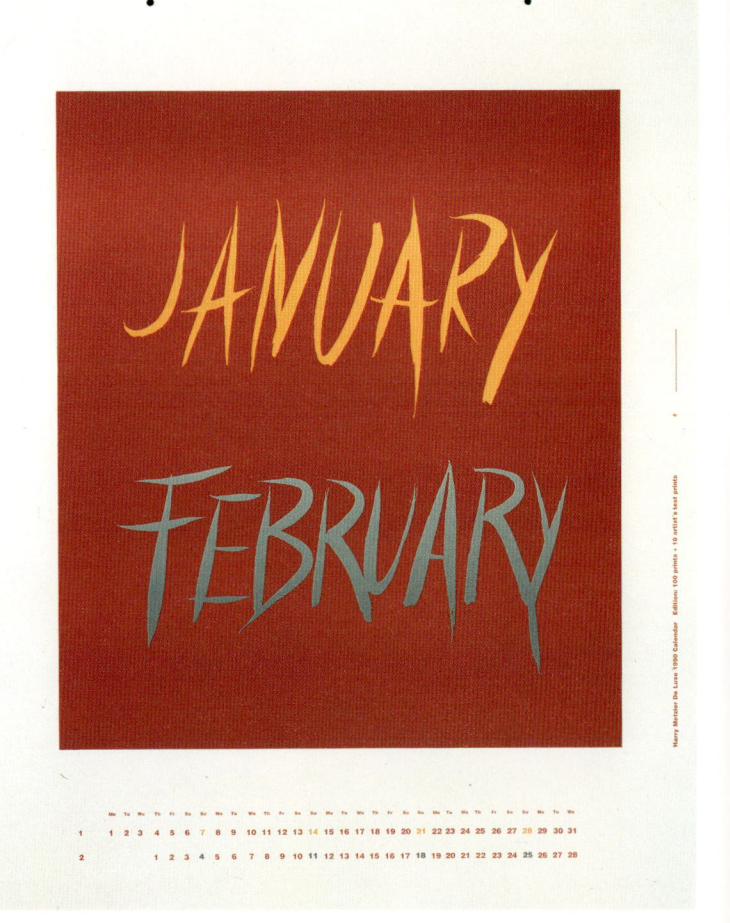

Born in Dornbirn, Austria, Harry Metzler studied graphic design in Graphische Bundes-Lehr-und Versuchsanstalt and Hochschule fur angewandte Kunst in Vienna. He also studied at the University of California, Los Angeles in the Department of Art. He traveled to Japan in 1978 and worked at the Takenobu Igarashi Design Studio, Tokyo.

harry metzler deluxe calendar

January
s m t w t f s
1 2 3 4 5
6 7 8 9 10 11 12
13 14 15 16 17 18 19
20 21 22 23 24 25 26
27 28 29 30 31

February
s m t w t f s
1 2
3 4 5 6 7 8 9
10 11 12 13 14 15 16
17 18 19 20 21 22 23
24 25 26 27 28

limited edition: 125 copies   1991

Earl Gee received his Bachelor's degree in graphic design with distinction from Art Center College of Design, Pasadena. He has also served on a United Nations sponsored delegation on package design touring the People's Republic of China. He established Earl Gee Design in 1990.

Greenleaf Medical
Hand Clinic Poster
Designer
Earl Gee
Design Firm
Earl Gee Design, California
Photographer
Geoffrey Nelson

FRED/ALAN INC.

MTV "Too Enormous"
Phone Kiosk Ad
Art Director
Tom Godici
Illustrator
Paul Corio
Design Firm
Fred/Alan Inc., New York

YOU CAN'T OUTGROW IT.
IT'S TOO ENORMOUS.

STYLISM

he work of Dean Morris has appeared in competitions sponsored by AIGA, ADC/NY, *Print*, and *ID Magazine*. A graduate of Cooper Union School of Art, he started Stylism, a graphic design studio in 1984. He has produced a line of recycled stationery, cards and giftwrap appearing under the Stylism name in gift and stationery stores nationwide. Having worked on various book projects and direct response television spots, he has taught at Cooper Union School of Art as well as Pratt Graduate Design School.

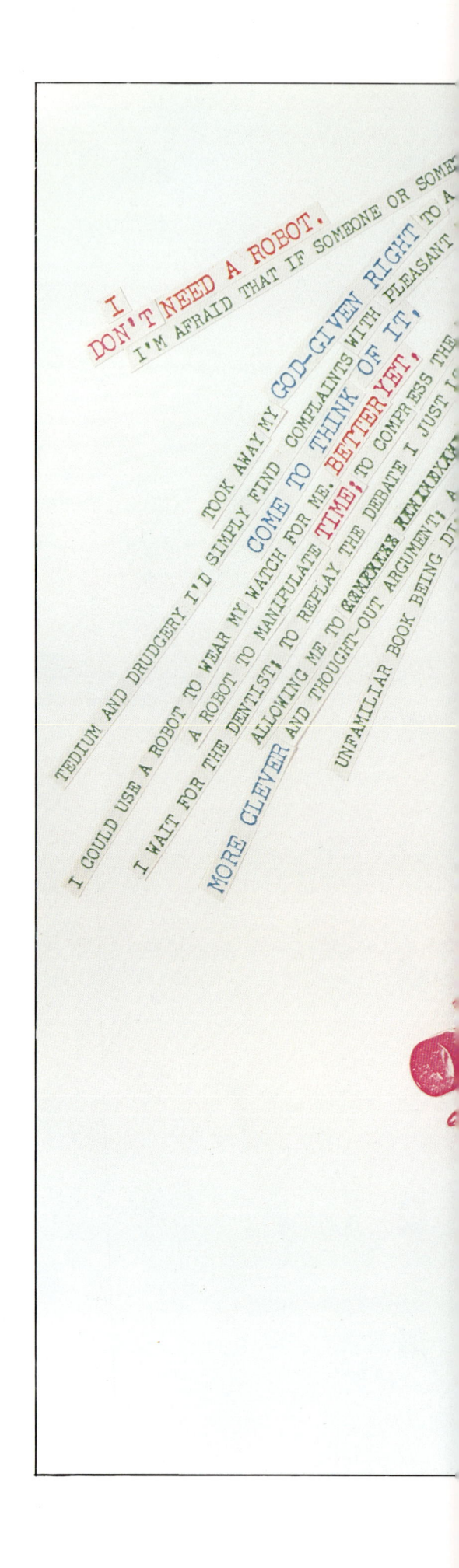

I DON'T NEED A ROBOT. I'M AFRAID THAT IF SOMEONE OR SOMETHING TOOK AWAY MY GOD-GIVEN RIGHT TO A TEDIUM AND DRUDGERY I'D SIMPLY FIND COMPLAINTS WITH PLEASANT I COULD USE A ROBOT TO WEAR MY WATCH FOR ME. COME TO THINK OF IT, A ROBOT TO MANIPULATE TIME; BETTER YET, I WAIT FOR THE DENTIST; TO COMPRESS THE ALLOWING ME TO REPLAY THE DEBATE I JUST MORE CLEVER AND THOUGHT-OUT ARGUMENT; UNFAMILIAR BOOK BEING D

I Don't Want A Robot
Designer
Dean Morris
Design Firm
Stylism, New York

DOUGLAS DESIGN OFFICE

"Shopping Bag Aux Sakawa"
Designer
Douglas Doolittle
Design Firm
Douglas Design Office
Photographer
Mizukoshi

Mikuwi's Wedding Poster
Designer
Douglas Doolittle
Design Firm
Douglas Design Office
Photographer
Nakamura

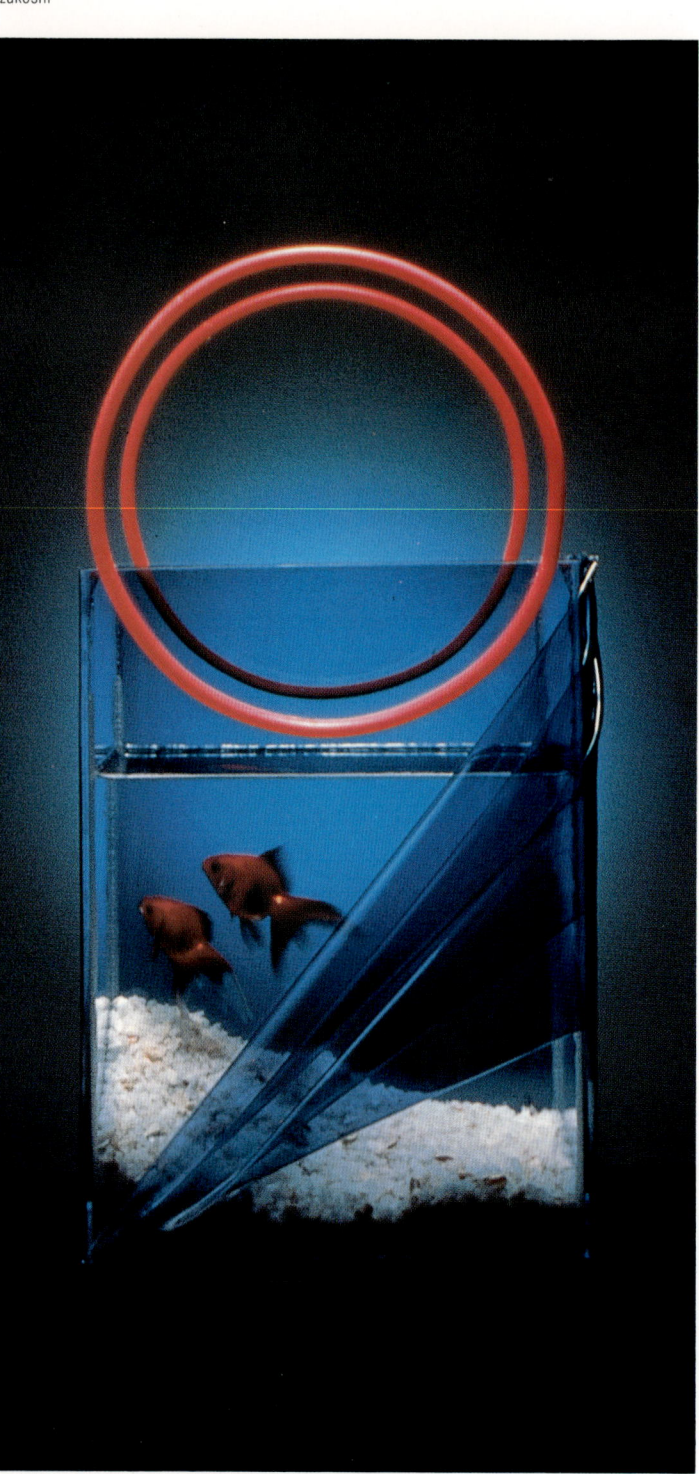

Born in Canada, Douglas Doolittle graduated from Sheridan College of Arts with a degree in graphic design. After working in Toronto he went to Europe to conduct research on a thesis dealing with the integration of culture and design. Introduced to G.K. Industrial Design Associates through Mr. Takenobu, he later worked there for two and a half years on corporate identity, signage and packaging projects. In 1979 he established Douglas Design Office in Tokyo concentrating on corporate identity projects. In 1991 he established Douglas Design. His work has appeared in over 40 publications throughout the world.

寿
Mr. Kiyomi Mikuni and his bride to be Miss Kumiko Amano will be joined together by the strings of harmonious matrimony. Mr. Mikuni, a renowned chef throughout Japan in the world of french cuisine along with the collaboration of numerous individuals have prepared a wedding reception of extravagant proportions; champagne not to mention, a vast array of food to be highlighted with several of Tokyo's top musicians are just some of the things that will make this event one to be always remembered. The reception will be held in the Fujinoma Suite of the Tokyo Imperial Hotel, Honkan. The evenings activities will commence from 6:30 in the evening on October, 20th. We look forward to seeing you.

SHIN MATSUNAGA DESIGN

Born in Tokyo in 1940, Shin Matsunaga graduated from the Tokyo National University of Fine Arts and Music in 1964. He established Shin Matsunaga Design Inc. in 1971. He has held one-man shows in Warsaw, Yugoslavia, New York, and Puerto Rico. His work encompasses a wide range of graphic design including poster, corporate identity, environmental as well as package design. His book *"The Design Works of Shin Matsunaga"* was published in 1992.

Kibun Sozai Can
Designer
Shin Matsunaga
Design Firm
Shin Matsunaga Design Inc., Tokyo

125

SHIN MATSUNAGA DESIGN

Art and Revolution
in Russia II
Designer
Shin Matsunaga
Design Firm
Shin Matsunaga Design Inc., Tokyo

Senden Kaigi
Designer
Shin Matsunaga
Design Firm
Shin Matsunaga Design Inc., Tokyo

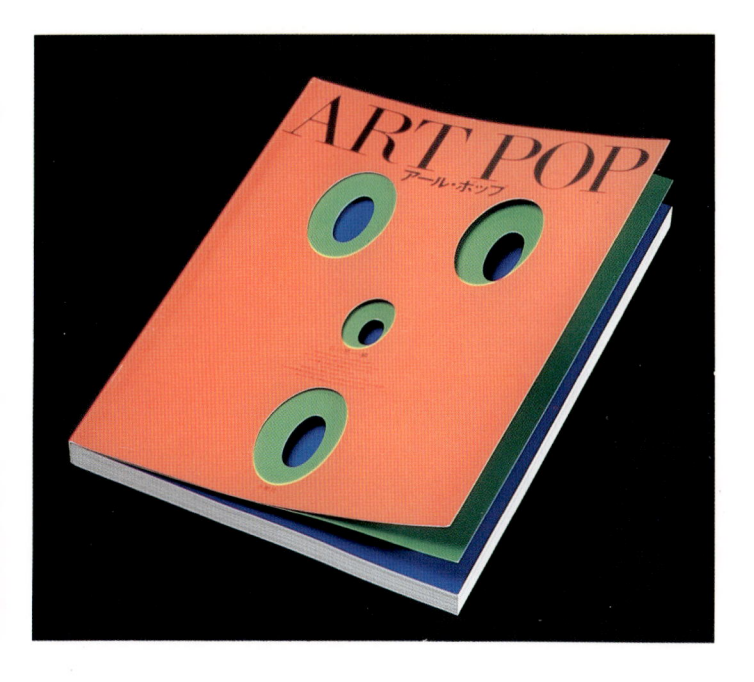

Art Pop
Designer
Shin Matsunaga
Design Firm
Shin Matsunaga Design Inc., Tokyo

ESKIND WADDELL

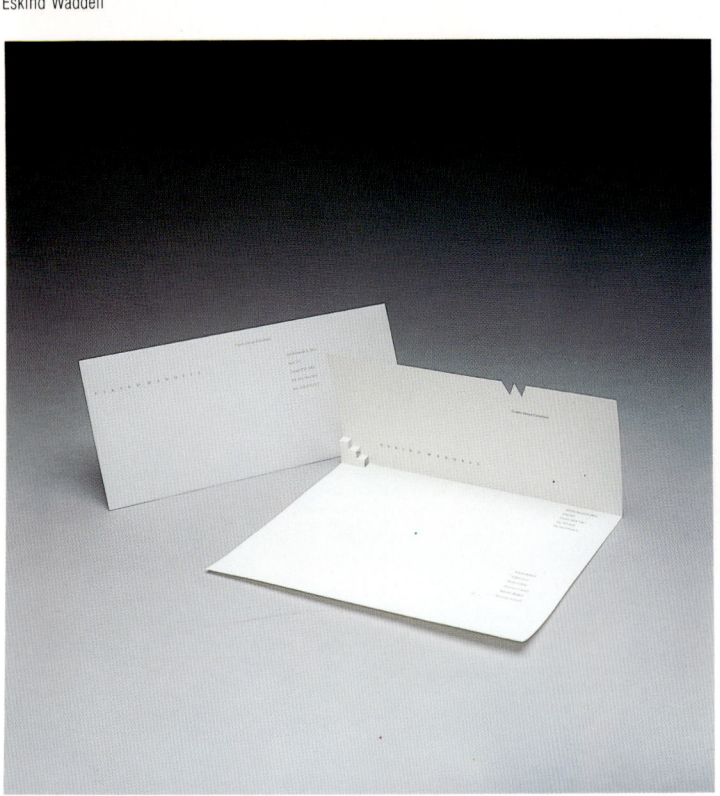

Signature Promotion for Mead
Design Firm
Eskind Waddell

Photo: Bob Anderson

Eskind Waddell Stationery
Designers
Christopher Campbell,
Roslyn Eskind
and Malcolm Waddell
Design Firm
Eskind Waddell

*e*skind studied in New York and graduated from the Cooper Union, School of Architecture before returning to Toronto. The British born Waddell was educated in England and trained in London and Montreal before finding his way to Toronto. The firm was born in 1975. From that time on their two separate biographies were combined to create Eskind Waddell. The firm has made a home in Toronto's business core focusing its energies on developing design solutions for a demanding corporate clientele. Over the firm's lifetime, these solutions have encompassed the entire breadth of corporate communications, from major publications like annual reports to the most fundamental element—the logo. It is a small, close-knit, collegial group of senior designers, "who individually and collectively bring one objective to every assignment—doing good work for clients."

129

Richard Seireeni studied architecture at the University of Washington. He has served as Associate Art Director of *Rolling Stone*, Studio Manager of Rod Dyer, Inc. and Creative Director of Warner Brothers Records, Inc. In 1984 he began his own business with the partnership of Vigon Seireeni. Today, that business continues as Studio Seireeni with a broad range of clients in a broad range of industries worldwide.

EARTH
LIFE
ANIMAL
POWER
GOTCHA

Gotcha
Earth Life Animal Power
Designer
Richard Seireeni
Design Firm
Vigon Seireeni, California
Photographer
Peggy Sirota

Gotcha
A Day In The Life
Of A Girl
Designer
Richard Seirenni
Design Firm
Vigon Seireeni, California
Photographer
Phillip Dixon

STUDIO SEIREENI

Kata
Designer
Romane Cameron
Design Firm
Studio Seireeni, California
Photographer
Amedeo

The New England
Holocaust Memorial
Competition
Designer
Anita Meyer
Design Firm
plus design inc., Massachusetts

"*Design is not a matter of simply deciding to make something traditional or non-traditional; design should respond to the client's objectives and budget. Our design solutions are the result of collaborating with our clients. Accepting a "non-traditional" design is not difficult for a client when the solution is an appropriate response to the project's criteria.*"

Alcan Architecture 1990
Designer
Anita Meyer
Design Firm
plus design inc., Massachusetts

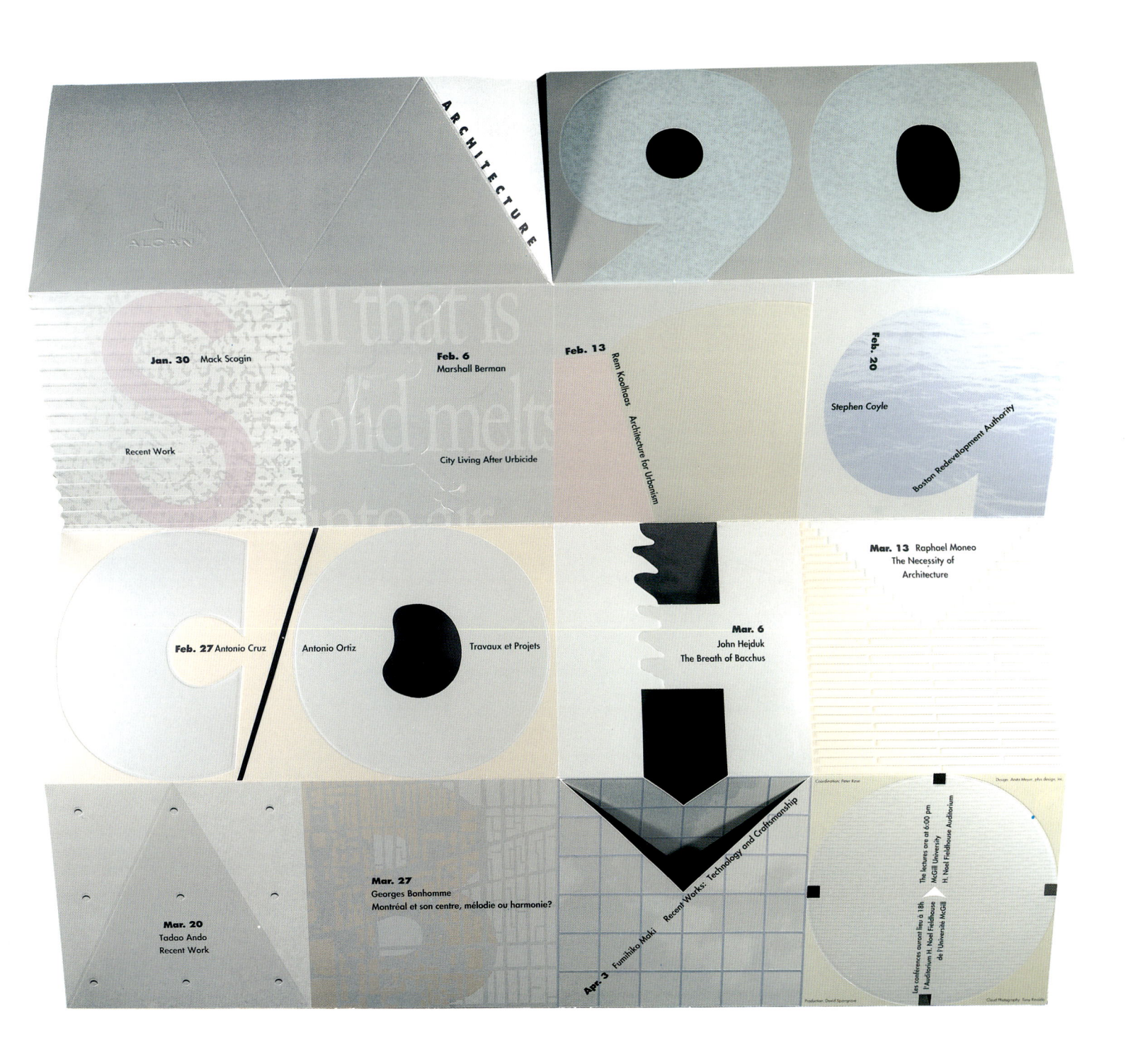

ARCHITECTURE

Jan. 30 Mack Scogin
Recent Work

Feb. 6 Marshall Berman
City Living After Urbicide

Feb. 13 Rem Koolhaas
Architecture for Urbanism

Feb. 20 Stephen Coyle
Boston Redevelopment Authority

Feb. 27 Antonio Cruz Antonio Ortiz
Travaux et Projets

Mar. 6 John Hejduk
The Breath of Bacchus

Mar. 13 Raphael Moneo
The Necessity of Architecture

Mar. 20 Tadao Ando
Recent Work

Mar. 27 Georges Bonhomme
Montréal et son centre, mélodie ou harmonie?

Apr. 3 Fumihiko Maki
Recent Works: Technology and Craftsmanship

Coordination: Peter Rose
Design: Arato Mayer, pfvs design, Inc.
Production: David Sparrgrove
Cloud Photography: Tony Rinaldo

The lectures are at 6:00 pm
H. Noël Fieldhouse Auditorium
McGill University

Les conférences auront lieu à 18h
l'Auditorium H. Noël Fieldhouse
de l'Université McGill

135

PARTNERS DESIGN GROUP

Shaun Dew's award-winning career began while she was still a student taking a post graduate degree in graphic design at the Royal College of Art. She joined the firm on its formation and became a partner in 1985.

After leaving the Royal College of Art Stephen Gibbons had his work selected for "Design and Art Direction" every year. He was invited to join The Partners as a senior designer and became a partner in 1985.

David Kimpton joined the partners in 1986 from Somerset College of Art, while Martin McLoughlin and Gareth Howat joined in 1988 from Preston Polytechnic and Kingston Polytechnic respectively.

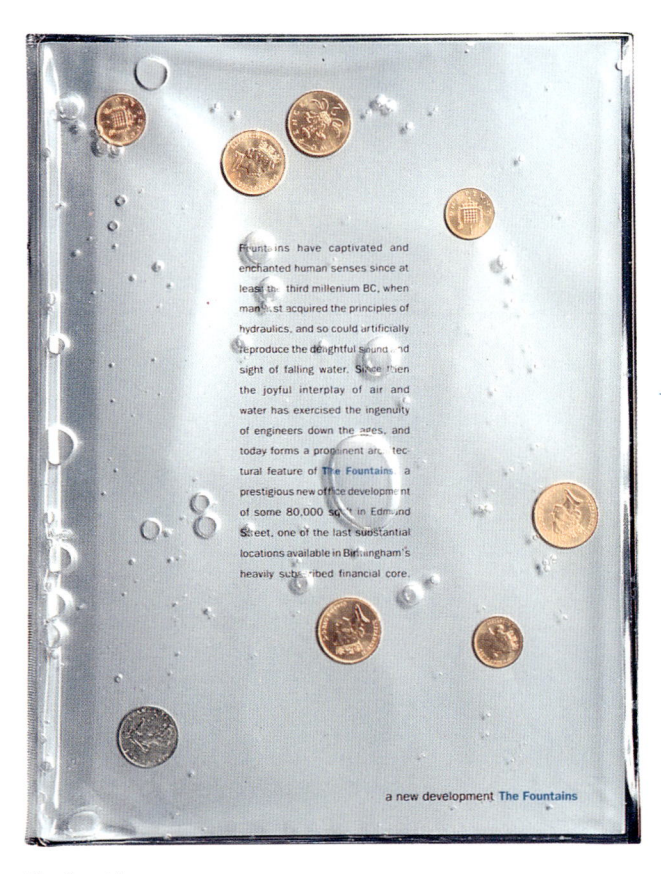

The Fountains
Designers
Martin McLoughlin and David Kimpton
Copywriting
Simon Rodway
Design Firm
The Partners
Design Consultants Ltd., London

The Royal Mail
First Review
Designer
Gareth Howat
Design Firm
The Partners
Design Consultants Ltd., London
Photographer
John Edwards

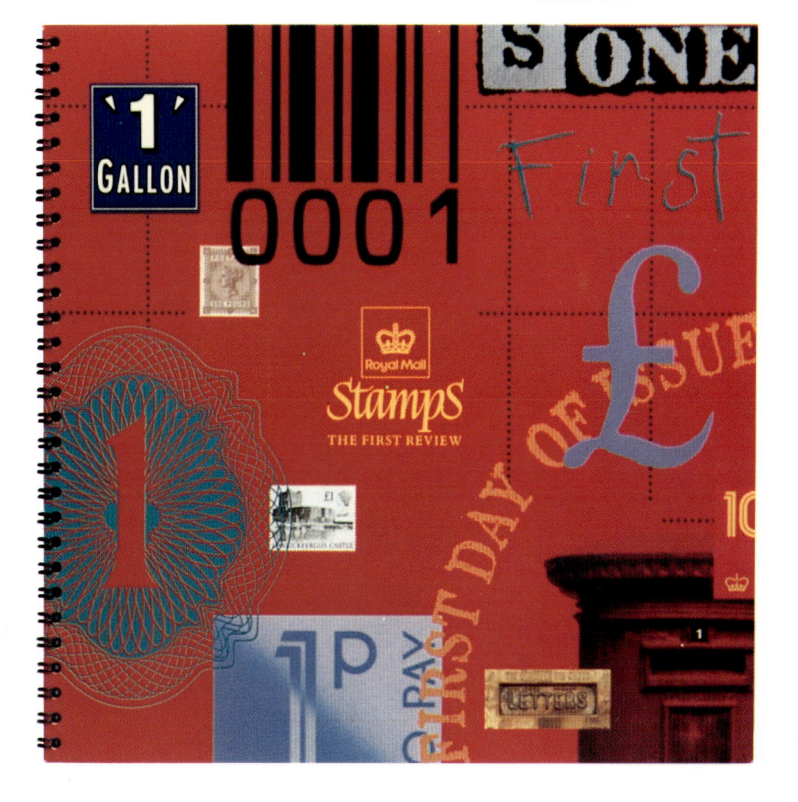

SIBLEY/PETEET

A native Texan, Don Sibley raises Bull Terriers and plays rhythm guitar for the Fabulous Fuzztones. He received a Bachelor of Fine Arts degree from Stephen F. Austin University in 1974. After working for several Dallas advertising and design firms he formed Sibley/Peteet Design in 1982 with partner Rex Peteet. His work has been published in *CA Magazine*, *Graphis*, *Print*, and *Idea Magazine*. His works are also in the Library of Congress and the Museum of Modern Art in Hiroshima.

Weyerhauser Paper
Promotion For Jaguar
Designer
Don Sibley
Printer
Williamson Printing
Design Firm
Sibley/Peteet Design, Texas

CATTING ABOUT BEGAN
WITH THE TOM CAT.
THE PROMISCUOUS PUSS RENOWNED FOR ITS
PROPENSITY TO PROWL.
THIS INFAMOUS FELINE IS FOREVER WHIRING AND
DIRING IN ITS QUEST
FOR FEMALE FRATERNITY. IN ONE CAT'S COMPANY
AND OUT ANOTHER, THE
TOM CAT HOLDS THE CONSTANTLY-BROKEN
RECORD FOR PROMISES
AND HEARTS.

TOM·CAT

Ever the smooth operator, Jaguar handles four-color process effortlessly.
And its bulk and opacity give Jaguar the performance qualities of a real heavyweight.

RICO LINS

MTV Breakthrough
Video Award
Designer
Rico Lins
Design Firm
Rico Lins Studio, New York
Photographer
Katherine McGlynn

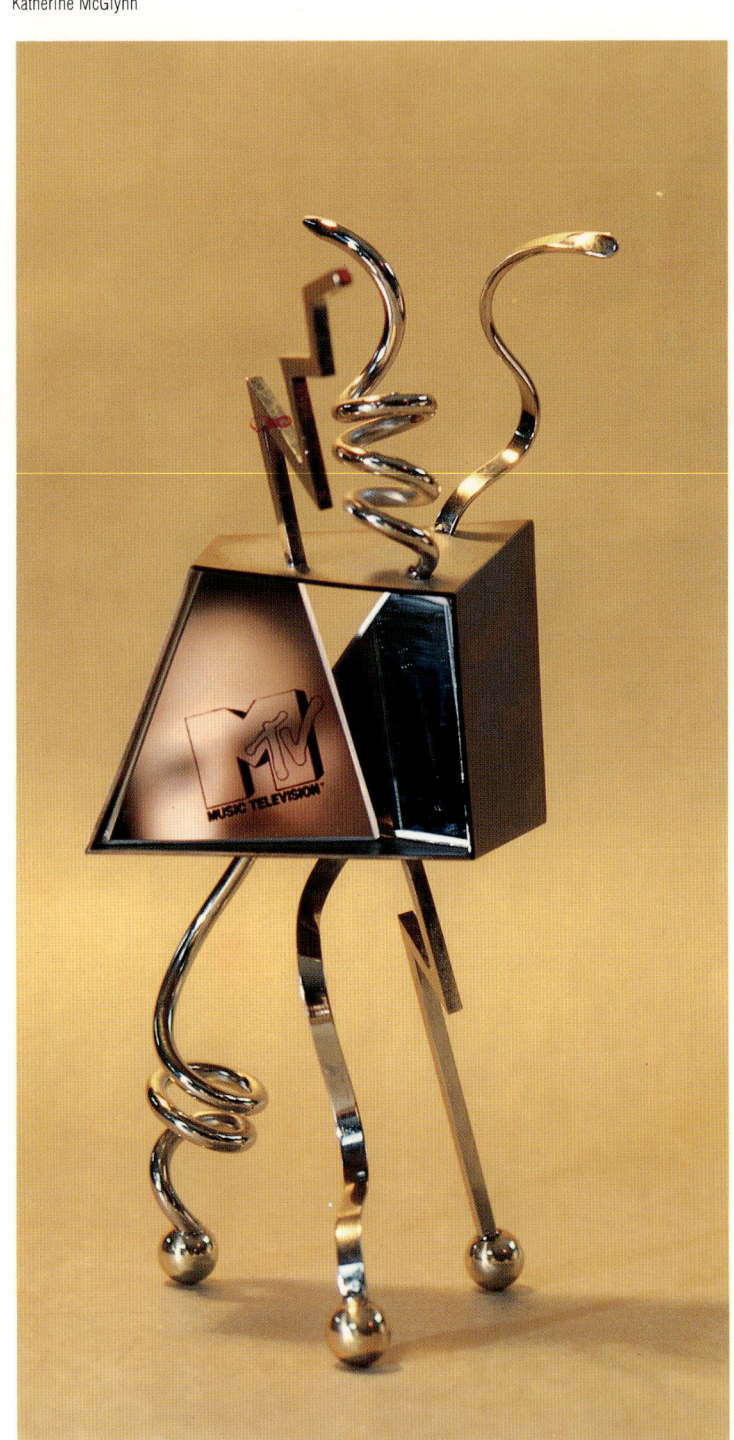

Born in Rio de Janeiro, Rico Lins has been working as a freelance illustrator and designer since 1976. Between 1979 and 1984 he lived in Paris where he was a regular contributor to such publications as *Le Monde, Revolution, Liberation, L'Expansion* and illustrated several book covers and children's books for Gallimard, Hachette, La Farandole and Amitie. In 1985 he returned to Rio de Janeiro where he designed and illustrated several posters, record jackets and magazine covers. Since he left his position as Art Director for CBS Records in New York he has been running his own studio where he develops freelance projects for MTV Networks, BMG, PolyGram, CTI and RCA Records.

"21 Bienal International
De São Paulo"
Designer
Rico Lins
Design Firm
Rico Lins Studio, New York
Photographer
Alejandro Cabrera

Around Dada
A Retrospective on Dadaism
Designer
Rico Lins
Design Firm
Rico Lins Studio, New York
Photographer
Rico Lins

"Kultur Revolution"
Designer
Rico Lins
Design Firm
Rico Lins Studio, New York
Photographer
Andre Ke

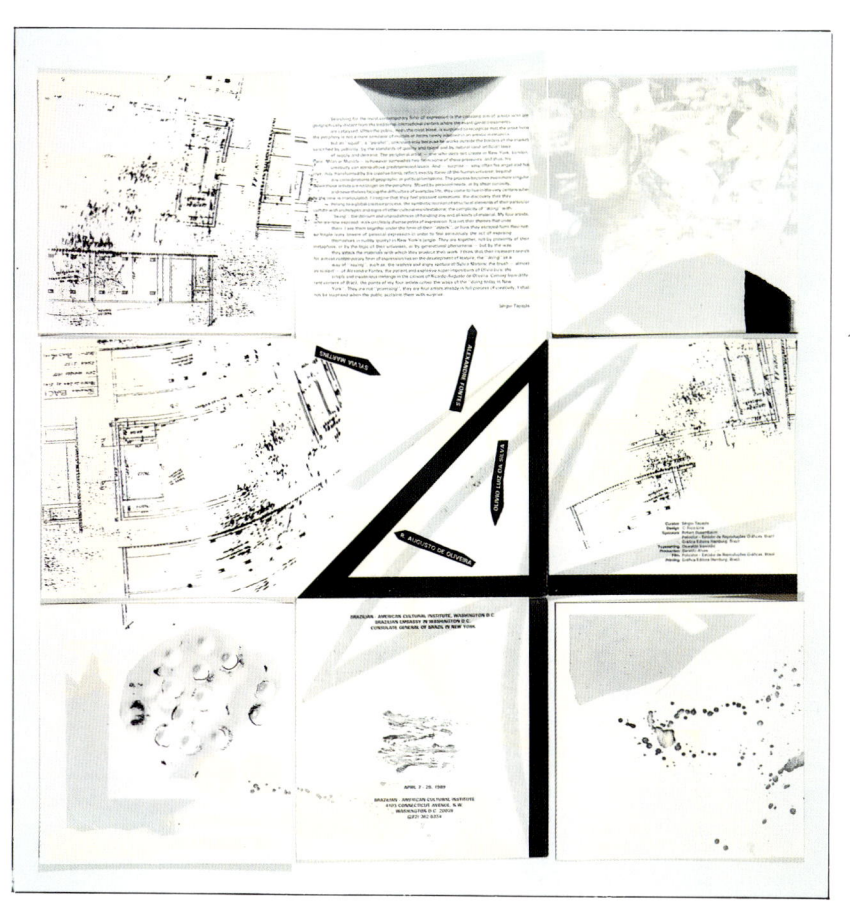

One-Piece Poster/
Invitation/
Promo For Art Exhibition
Designer
Rico Lins
Design Firm
Rico Lins Studio, New York

B J KRIVANEK

Art Directors Club
of Los Angeles Show
Exhibition
Designer, Design Director
B J Krivanek
Multimedia Producer
Bill Maddox
Lighting Coordinator
Todd M. Vey
Exhibition Coordinators
Mark Gilmour and Tom Rogers
Show Chairperson
Silvija Zemjanis
Judging Coordinator
Vickie Goodale Sparks
Design Firm
B J Krivanek Art + Design,
California

"*The design of the invitation aestheticized kitsch elements in 3D to be viewed with red/blue 3D glasses, proving that good design can rescue anything from ugliness. Indeed, this was the collective ideolgy of the design team—us pop cultural noise and we can make pop cultural music.*"

Art Directors Club of Los Angeles Show Call-for-Entries Poster
Designers
Mark Gilmour, BJ Krivanek, Tom Rogers
Design Firm
B J Krivanek Art + Design, California
Photographer
Rosanne Fett

Art Directors Club of Los Angeles Show Opening Invitation
Designer
B J Krivanek
Design Firm
B J Krivanek Art + Design, California
Photographer
Rosanne Fett

145

MTV CREATIVE SERVICES

1989 MTV
Video Music Awards Book
Designer
Stacy Drummond and Steve Byram
Illustrator
Steve Byram
Design Firm
MTV Networks Creative Services,
New York

Stacy Drummond is a graphic designer, illustrator, furniture designer, and landscape designer. She studied printmaking for three years at Penn State, and graphic design for three years at Pratt Institute.

Born in Oakland, California in 1952, Stephen Byram studied art at the Academy of Art in San Francisco. In 1979 he moved to New York, and has been working in the music business ever since. During those years some of his most memorable moments have occurred while collaborating with Stacy Drummond.

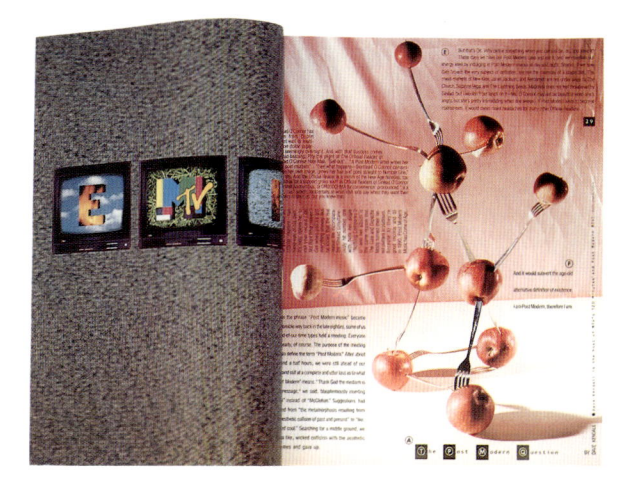

1990 MTV
Video Music Awards Book
Designers
Stacy Drummond and Steve Byram
Design Firm
MTV Networks Creative Services,
New York

❝ True friends are rare, true collaborators more so. I've been fortunate. ❞

❝ What I try to do is design like a painter. Given the times we're in, that's considered alternative, to me it's just natural. ❞

❝ The reason for non-traditional design is the need for the non-traditional. It may look easy but it's not. This is something a lot of designers do not choose to understand. ❞

147

1991 MTV
Video Music Awards Book
Designers
Stacy Drummond and Steve Byram
Illustrator
Khauled
Design Firm
MTV Networks Creative Services,
New York

MTV CREATIVE SERVICES

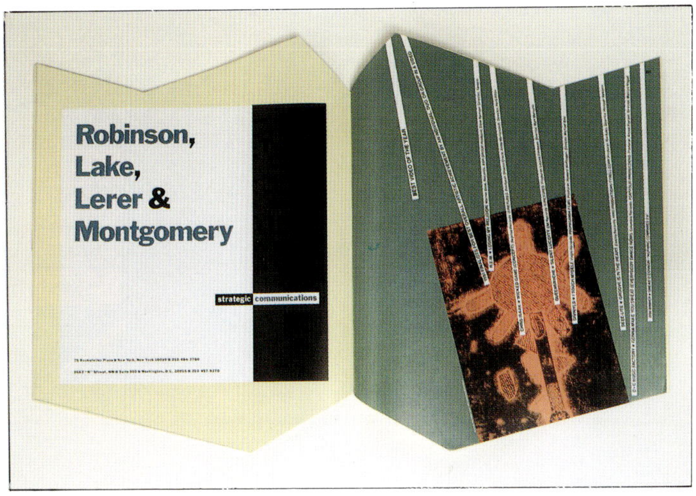
Robinson,
Lake,
Lerer &
Montgomery
strategic communications

15
in a dream
you saw a
way to survive
and you were
full of joy

METROPOLIS

Metropolis Magazine,
December 1990
Designers
Nancy Cohen and Carl Lehmann-Haupt
Design Firm
Metropolis

museums customarily display design as if it were art. now, curators are trying to take design objects off their pedestals and out of their glass cases.

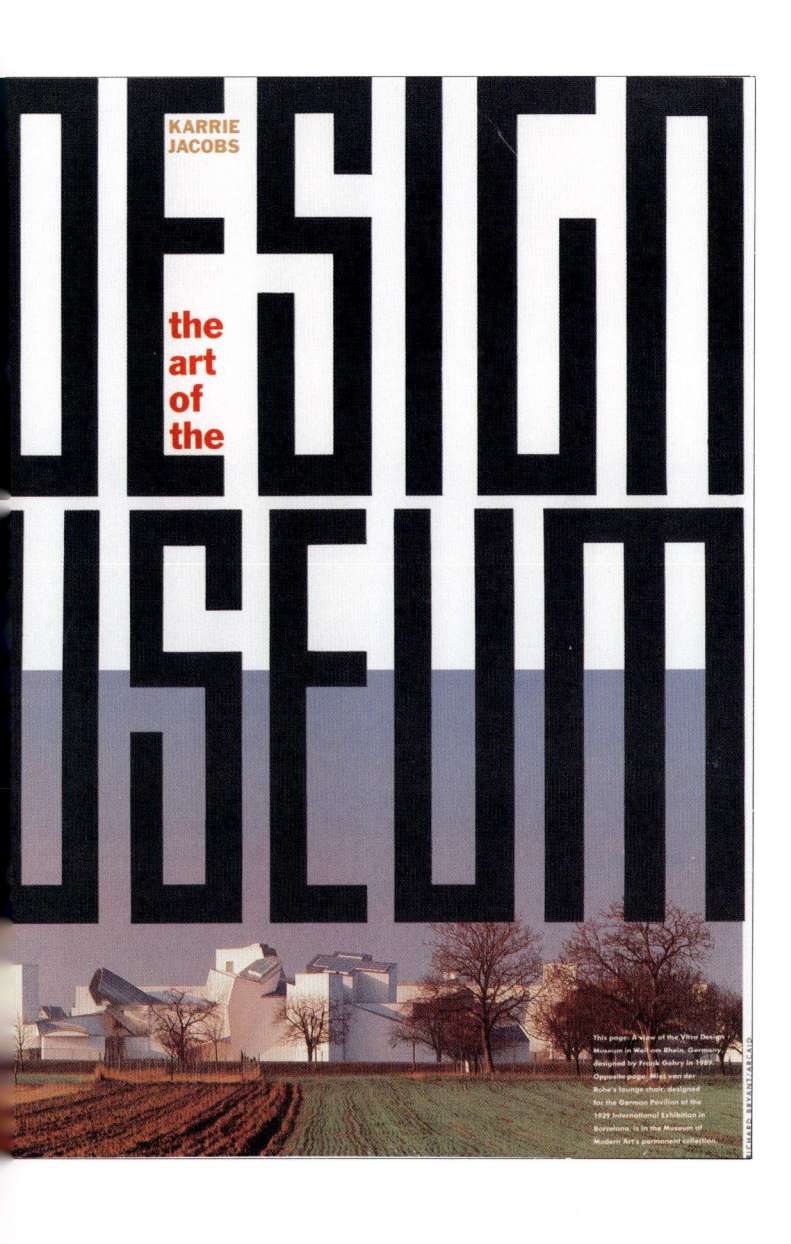

Metropolis Magazine,
April 1991
Designers
Nancy Cohen and Carl Lehmann-Haupt
Design Firm
Metropolis

GARY PANTER

as the head production designer for "Pee-Wee's Playhouse" Gary Panter received three Emmy Awards for design. Born in 1950 in Durant, Oklahoma, he earned a Bachelor of Fine Arts at East Texas State University in 1974. He has taught and lectured at schools throughout the world. His paintings have been shown in exhibitions in New Orleans, Tokyo, Pensacola and New York and featured in publications such as *Esquire*, *Spy*, and *Entertainment Weekly*. He has designed everything from billboards to the Children's Playroom at the Paramount Hotel.

"One Hell Soundwich"
Designers
Frank Gargiulo and Helene Silverman
Illustrators
Jay Cotton and Gary Panter
Photographer
Kristine Larsen
Design Firm
Hello Studio, New York

153

The Red Hot Chili Peppers
The Uplift Mofo Party Plan
Designer
Henry Marquez
Illustrator
Gary Panter

GARY PANTER

Frank Zappa
Studio Tan
Designer
Vartan
Illustrator
Gary Panter

Logo Bromide for Paco's Flowers
Designers
Alan Chan, Phillip Leung
Design Firm
Alan Chan Design Co., Wanchai, Hong Kong

The fusion of Oriental and Western cultures in contemporary graphic design is a dominant theme in Alan Chan's creative work. By combining the two, he has succeeded in creating his own unique style. Via this different perspective, he has contributed to a rediscovery and appreciation of traditional Chinese art and culture. In 1990, Alan Chan launched into product design with t-shirts, paper and tin products marketed in Hong Kong, Singapore, Taiwan, Japan, France, Germany and Canada. In addition he was commissioned by Nikko Company in Japan to create contemporary Chinese tableware designs.

Born in 1950, he is one of the few Hong Kong-trained graphic designers who have achieved international recognition. During his 20 years in advertising and design, he has won more than 200 local and international awards.

Logo Design for Stylistics
Designer
Alan Chan
Design Firm
Alan Chan Design Co., Wanchai, Hong Kong

Canton Discotheque
(Corporate Identity)
Designers
Alan Chan,
Alvin Chan, Phillip Leung
Illustrator
Terry Liu
Design Firm
Alan Chan Design Co.,
Wanchai, Hong Kong

JACOBS FULTON DESIGN

Annual Report
Designer
Clay Williams
Design Firm
Jacobs Fulton Design Group, California
© 1991 Cadence Design Systems, Inc.

159

DAVID CARSON DESIGN

David Carson was teaching high school sociology and psychology when he got a brochure in the mail urging him to attend a two-week workshop at the University of Arizona to study graphic design. He signed up and soon discovered what he wanted to do with the rest of his life. Later, while enrolled at Ashland College of Commercial Art in Ashland, Oregon a friend at Surfer Publications suggested he send his work to the art director. Carson parlayed this connection into an internship and he has been working in the field ever since.*

*Paraphrased from Step-By-Step Graphics.

pRETTY 4

PICTURES FROM

EUROPE

"*Ultimately, one's influences as a designer must come from within. The strongest, most emotional work springs from utilizing your own unique background, personality and life experiences. When you combine these with observations from the world around you, your supply of influences and ideas are limitless.*"

Beach Culture Magazine
Issue 5
Designer
David Carson
Design Firm
David Carson Design, California

R

LAST NIGHT BEFORE

161

Beach Culture Magazine
Issue 4
Designer
David Carson
Design Firm
David Carson Design, California

UNCOVERED! A PEEK AT BATHING SUITS PAST AND PRESENT, AND WHY THE B

DAVID CARSON DESIGN

THE SAME WITHOUT THEM

what's all this noise about anyway? wha
t's all **this_noise about**
WHAT'S ALL THIS NOISE ABOUT ANYWAY? bout anyway?
lyle lovett photo by al an messer

Beach Culture Magazine
Issue 3
Designer
David Carson
Design Firm
David Carson Design, California

163

MARIA GRILLO

A graduate of the University of Illinois, Maria Grillo became a principal in the design firm VSA Partners in 1991. Her work has been recognized by a variety of publications and competitions, including *Print*, and *ID* magazines and the American Center for Design 100 Show. She is an AIGA/Chicago executive board member.

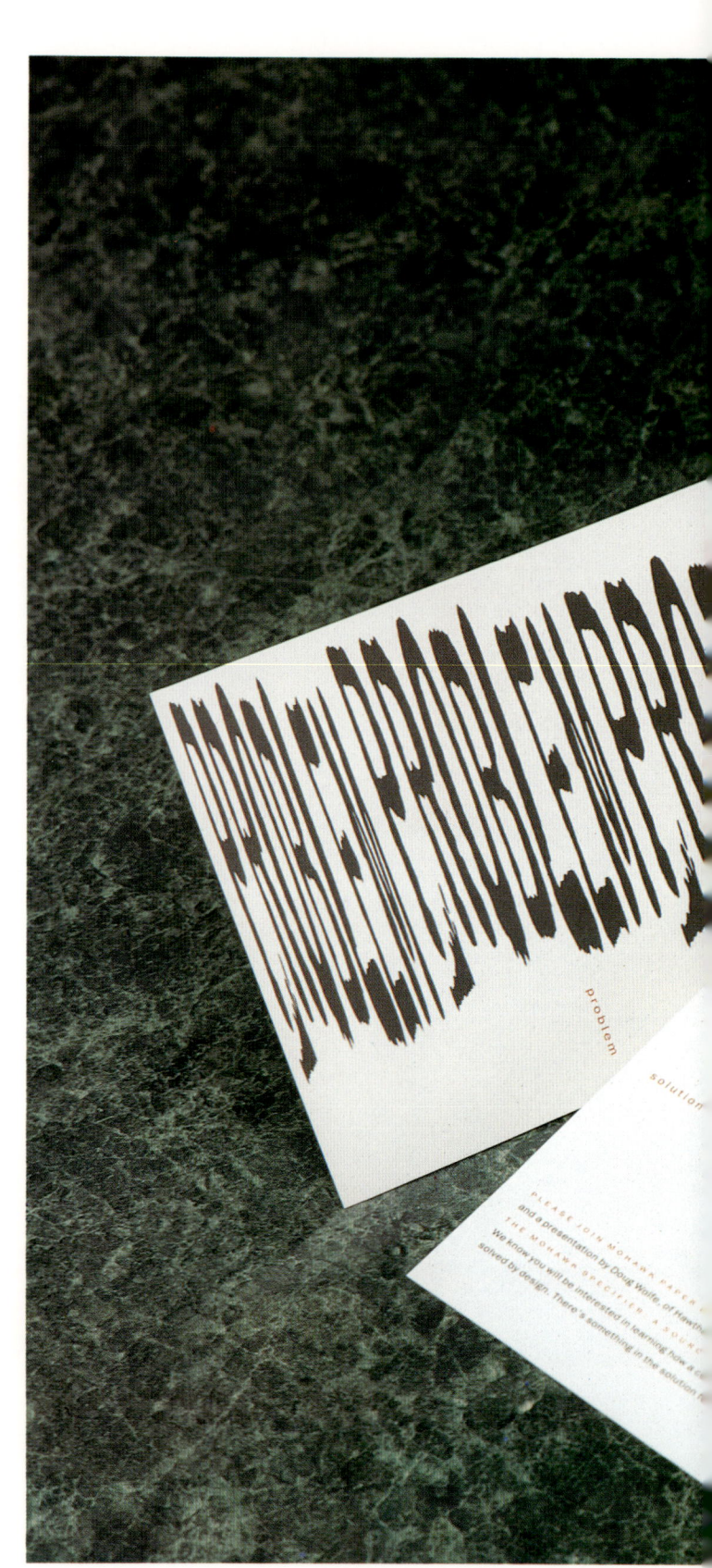

Mohawk
Designer
Maria Grillo
Design Firm
Maria Grillo Design, Illinois
Photographer
Maria Grillo

AR 100 Show
Call for Entries
Designer
Janet Giampietro
Design Firm
Black Book Marketing Group
Illustrator
Jeffrey Fisher

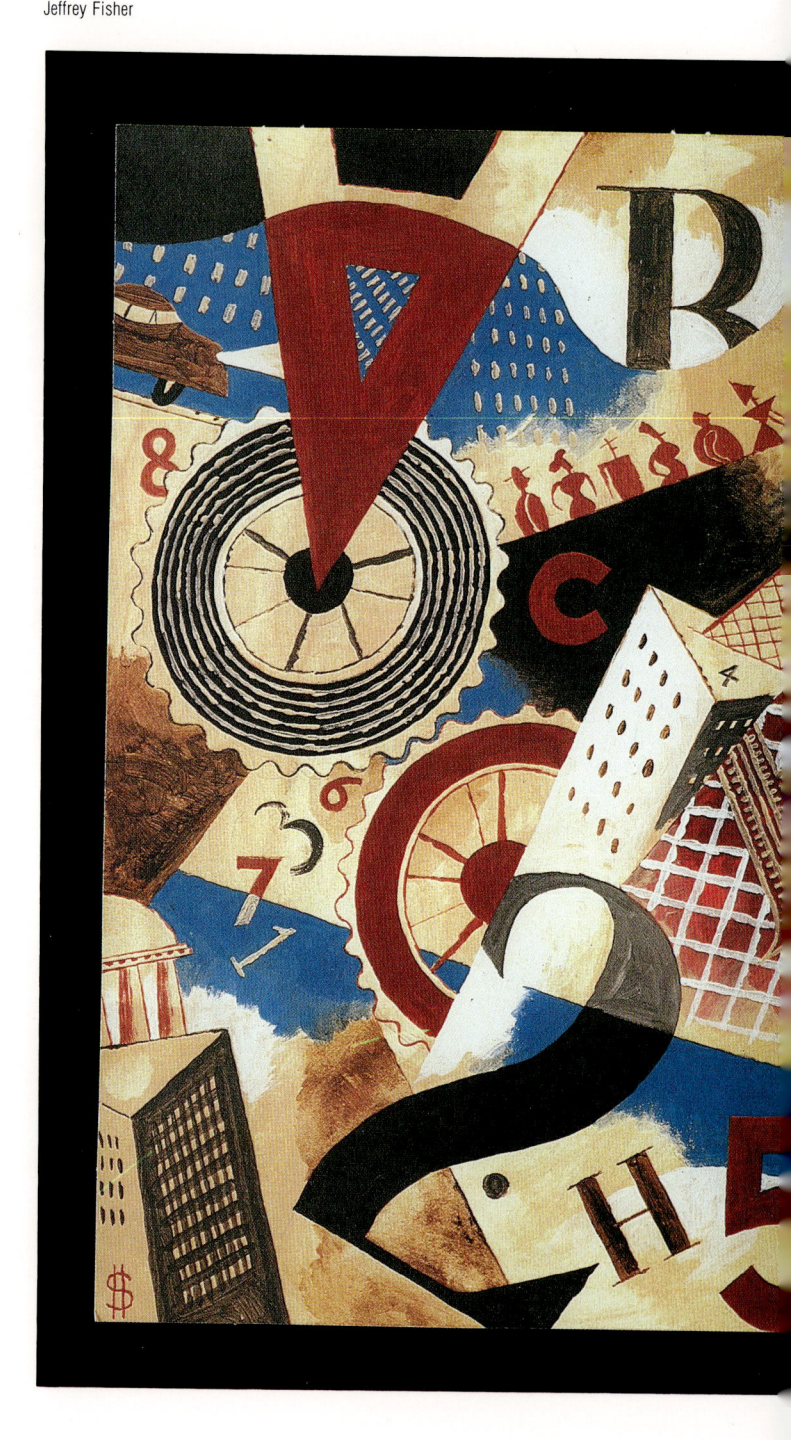

Upon my graduation from the Philadelphia College of Art with a degree in Graphic Design, my desire to have my own clients proved stronger than the lure of the great design studios of New York. Studio Francesca was the result. Since then, my studio has grown and benefitted from the experience I've gained working with a broad diversity of clients, including most recently, the Black Book Marketing Group.

"My passions for world travel, art history and tactile modes of expression such as bookbinding and origami lend creative solutions to my strongest promotional projects. Unexpected shapes, folds and unique juxtaposition of materials make for solutions that are more interactive and memorable—and therefore, more successful."

!?

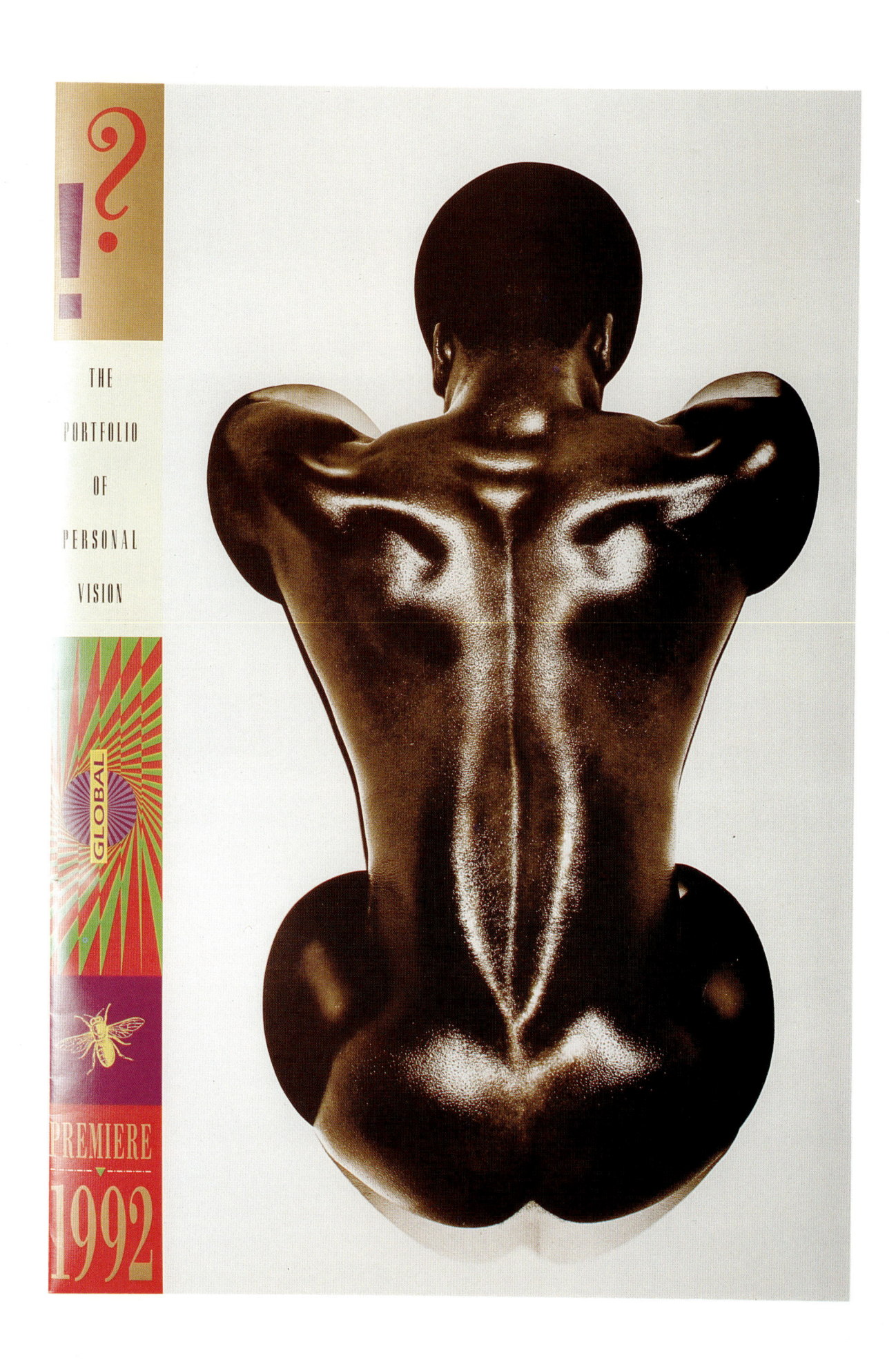

THE
PORTFOLIO
OF
PERSONAL
VISION

GLOBAL

PREMIERE
1992

CREATIVE BLACK BOOK

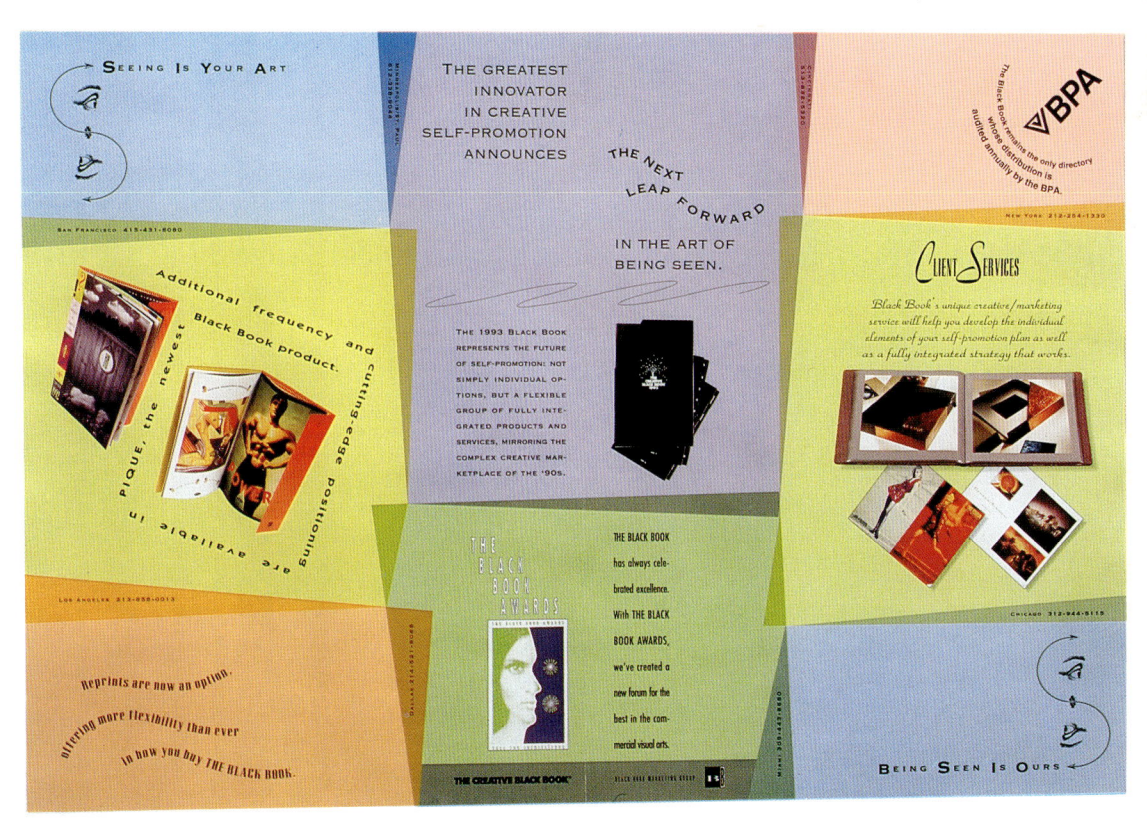

Pique—Portfolio
of Personal Vision
Design Firm
Black Book Marketing Group

EMIGRE GRAPHICS

Vanderlans was born in 1955 in The Hague, Holland. From 1975–1979, he studied graphic design at the Royal Academy of Fine Art, and from 1981–1982, studied photography at U.C. Berkeley. In 1986, together with his wife and business partner, Zuzana Licko Vanderlans, he founded Emigre Magazine, a journal for experimental graphic design. As a graphic design team, Emigre has worked for clients including Apple Computer, Adobe Systems, San Francisco Artspace, Macworld and MacWeek, among several others. Their work has been published in various design publications throughout the United States and Europe, while select pieces of their work appear in the permanent collections of respected museums throughout the world, including the San Francisco Museum of Modern Art and the Design Museum of London. Emigre's most recent addition, Emigre Music, is devoted to releasing contemporary music on compact discs and cassettes.

Super Collider Poster
Designer
Rudy Vanderlans
Design Firm
Emigre Graphics
Photographer
Bill McConnell

su per col li der

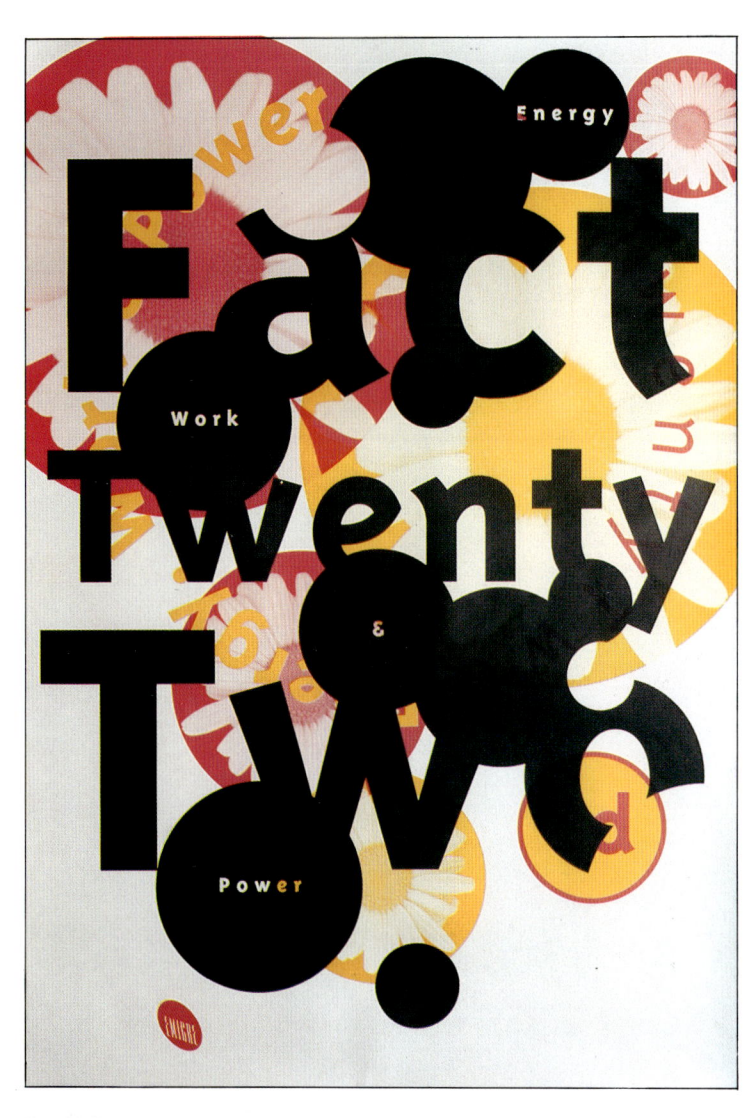

Fact 22 Poster
Designer
Rudy Vanderlans
Design Firm
Emigre Graphics
Photographer
Bill McConnell

Emigre Music
Designer
Rudy Vanderlans
Design Firm
Emigre Graphics
Photographer
Bill McConnell

171

RUSSO SICARD STUDIO

Region of Puglia Italy
Poster
Designers
Giovanni C. Russo
and Florence Sicard
Design Firm
Russo, Sicard Studio, New York

Todd Haiman
Photographer Advertisement
Designer
Giovanni C. Russo
Design Firm
Russo, Sicard Studio, New York
Photographer
Todd Haiman

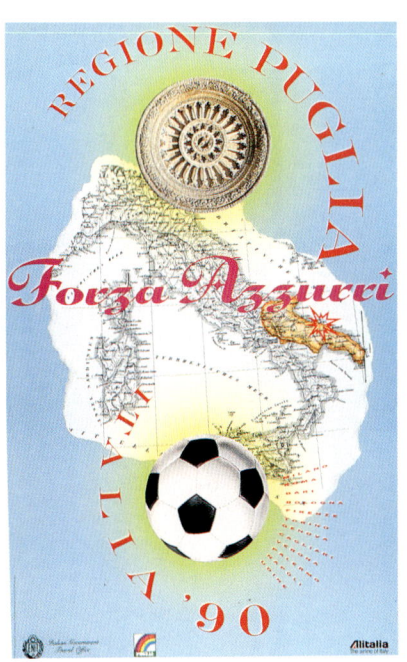

Region of Puglia,
"Italia 90" Soccer Poster
Designer
Giovanni C. Russo
Design Firm
Russo, Sicard Studio, New York

173

APPENDIX

2029
Photogalerie The Compagnie
Poolstrasse 7
D-2000 Hamburg 36

AGI
1950 N. Ruby Street
Melrose Park, IL 60160

Army Trainer Magazine
Drawer "A"
Fort Eustis, VA 23604

Blackdog Design
257A Miller Ave.
Mill Valley, CA 94941

Alan Chan
2/F Shiu Lam Bldg.
23 Luard Rd.
Wanchai, Hong Kong

Wing Chan
79 Barrow St. #6A
New York, NY 10014

Art Chantry
PO Box 4069
Seattle, WA 98104

Concrete
633 S. Plymouth Ct. #208
Chicago, IL 60605

Cranbrook Academy of Art
500 Lone Pine Rd. Box 801
Bloomfield Hills, MI 48303

Creative Black Book
115 Fifth Ave.
New York, NY 10003

David Carson Design
128½ 10th Street
Del Mar, CA 92104

Paul Davis
14 E. 4th Street
New York, NY 10012

Douglas Design Office
Shibuya-Ku
Kamiyama-Cho 12-7
Uchino Heights #201
Tokyo, Japan

Emigre Graphics
48 Shaituck Square No. 175
Berkeley, CA 94704

Faith
1179A King St. West #112
Toronto, Ontario, Canada M6K 3C5

Fred/Alan Inc.
708 Broadway 8th floor
New York, NY 10003

Earl Gee
501 Second St. #700
San Francisco, CA 94107

Milton Glaser
207 E. 32nd St.
New York, NY 10016

Granary Books
568 Broadway
New York, NY 10012

Maria Grillo
VSA Graphic Design
542 S. Dearborn, Suite 202
Chicago, IL 60605

Chris Harvey
MTV National Video Graphics
460 W. 42nd Street
New York, NY 10036

Allen Hori
HardWerken Design BV
PO Box 25058
3001 HB Rotterdam
The Netherlands

Hot House
52A Water St.
Vancouver, BC, Canada V6B 1A4

Ink Tank
2 W. 47th St.
New York, NY 10036

Alexander Isley
361 Broadway, Suite 111
New York, NY 10013

Jacobs Fulton Design
745 Emerson St.
Palo Alto, CA 94301

Chip Kidd
Random House Inc.
201 W. 50th Street
New York, NY 10022

BJ Krivanek
2050 Walgrove Ave.
Los Angeles, CA 90066

Frans Lieshout
Geesterduinweg 184
1902 CC Castricum
The Netherlands

Rico Lins
406 E. 13th St.
New York, NY 10009

M & Co.
50 W. 17th Street
New York, NY 10011

Anthony Ma
855 W. Blackhawk
Chicago, IL 60622

Shin Matsunaga Design
8F Ishibash Bldg.
7-3-1 Minami-Aoyama
Minato-Ku
Tokyo 107 Japan

Metropolis
177 E. 87th Street #504
New York, NY 10128

Harry Metzler
Brand 774
A-6867 Schwarzenberg
Austria

Michael Peters Ltd.
49 Princes Place
London W11 4QA

Corey Edmonds Millen
75 Varick St. 15th floor
New York, NY 10013

MTV Creative Services
1515 Broadway
New York, NY 10036

Nippon Design Center
Chuo-Daiwa Bldg.
1-13-13 Ginza Chuo-Ku
Tokyo 104 Japan

OLIO
9½ Wavecrest Ave.
Venice, CA 90291

Gary Panter
505 Court St. #75
Brooklyn, NY 11231

Paper Moon Graphics
PO Box 34672
Los Angeles, CA 90034

Partners Design Group
243 Riverside Drive
New York, NY 10025

plus design, inc.
10 Thatcher St. #109
Boston, MA 02113

Mike Quon Design Office
568 Broadway Rm. 703
New York, NY 10012

Jesse Reyes
Harris Publications
1115 Broadway 8th floor
New York, NY 10010

Javier Romero
9 W. 19th St. 5th floor
New York, NY 10011

Russo, Sicard Studio
307 E. 44th Street #1103
New York, NY 10017

Makoto Saito
#206 Flat-Aoyama
5-15-9 Minami Aoyama
Minato-Ku, Tokyo 107

Mike Salisbury
2200 Amapola Court
Torrance, CA 90501

Sibley/Peteet
965 Slocum
Dallas, TX 75207

Siebert Design
323 E. 8th Street
Cincinnati, OH 45202

Studio Seireeni
708 S. Orange Grove
Los Angeles, CA 90036

Stylism
307 E. 6th Street #4B
New York, NY 10003

Thirst
855 W. Blackhawk #203
Chicago, IL 60622

Edwin Torres
120 E. 4th Street
New York, NY 10003

Eskind Waddell
260 Richmond St. W. #201
Toronto, Canada M5V 1W5

Waters Design Associates Inc.
3 W. 18th Street
New York, NY 10011

Weller Institute for the Cure of Design
1398 Aerie Drive, Box 726
Park City, UT 84060

Worksight
611 Broadway Room 841
New York, NY 10012

Lloyd Ziff
55 Van Damst #904
New York, NY 10013

REFERENCES & SUGGESTED READING

Aldersey-Williams, Hugh *New American Design: Products and Graphics for a Post Industrial Age,* New York, Rizzoli International Publications, Inc., 1988.

Beylerian, George M. and Jeffrey J. Osborne, *Mondo Materialis: Materials and Ideas for the Future,* New York, Harry N. Abrams, Inc., 1990.

Bourdon, David, *Warhol,* New York, Harry N. Abrams, Inc., 1989.

Caplan, Ralph, *By Design,* New York, St Martin's Press, 1982.

Costantino, Mary, *Picasso Posters,* New York, Cresent Books, 1991.

Davis, Deborah, Jill Swanson Reddig, *Dictionary of Contemporary Quotations* John Gordon Burke Publishers, 1981.

Gosney, Michael, Linnea Dayton, Jennifer Ball, *The Verbum Book of Digital Typography,* Redwood, CA, M&T Books, 1991.

Igarashi, Takenobu, *Seven Graphic Designers,* Tokyo, Graphic-sha Publishing Company Ltd, 1985.

Labuz, Ronald, *Contemporary Graphic Design,* New York, Van Nostrand Reinhold, 1991.

Lupton, Ellen, *Graphic Design and Typography in The Netherlands: A View of Recent Work,* New York, The Cooper Union and Princeton Architectural Press, 1992.

Meggs, Philip, *History of Graphic Design,* New York, Van Nostrand Reinhold, 1992.

Novosedlik, Will "*Honor Among Thieves*" Applied Arts Quarterly Volume 6, Number 3, Fall 1991, Page 61–67.

Pater, Alan F. and Jason R. Pater, *What they said in 1990: The Year Book of World Opinion,* Palm Springs, CA: Monitor, 1991.

PRINT MAGAZINE (Dutch Issue), November/December 1991, Print XLV:VI

Radice, Barbara, *Memphis: Research, Experiences, Results, Failures and Successes of New Design,* New York, Rizzoli International Publications, Inc., 1984.

Rand, Paul, *Paul Rand: A Designer's Art.,* New Haven, CT, Yale University Press, 1985.

Wozencroft, Jon, *The Graphic Language of Neville Brody,* New York, Rizzoli International Publications, Inc., 1988.

ACKNOWLEDGMENTS

I ACKNOWLEDGE AND THANK THE MANY PEOPLE WHO GENEROUSLY CONTRIBUTED THEIR ENERGY, SUPPORT, TIME AND IDEAS IN HELPING MAKE THIS BOOK POSSIBLE. THEY INCLUDE: • SPECIAL THANKS TO MY EDITOR, KEVIN CLARK, FOR HIS HELP IN SHAPING THE FOCUS OF THIS BOOK. ALSO TO PENNY SIBAL, MARK SERCHUCK, RICHARD LIU, CARRIE ABEL, ANTHONY TRAMA, BEDELIA HILL AT PBC INTERNATIONAL FOR ALL THEIR ASSISTANCE. • APPRECIATION TO CHRISTINA WOO FOR HER RESEARCH, ENCOURAGEMENT AND SUPERB COACHING. • MY COLLEAGUES AT MIKE QUON DESIGN OFFICE — EILEEN KINNEARY FOR HER INVALUABLE DESIGN ASSISTANCE, STEVE NEWMAN, JIMMY LUI, PETER GATTO, MICHAEL FORD, TODD GILMORE, DAWN MORALES AND RON EDELSTEIN. • SINCEREST THANKS TO LES BARANY, LEW DOLIN, DAVID REVERE MCFADDEN/CURATOR OF DECORATIVE ARTS COOPER-HEWITT, NATIONAL MUSEUM OF DESIGN, IVAN PAK, ROBERT ENO STUDIO, NANCY ALDRICH-RUENZEL/EDITORIAL DIRECTOR-VICE PRESIDENT STEP BY STEP PUBLISHING, BRAD DONENFELD, NATHAN GLUCK/A.I.G.A., KATHERINE MCCOY, GARY PANTER, SCOTT SANTORO, EVE MICHEL, TONY CICCOLELLA, DEAN MORRIS, JUDY RADICE, SCOTT KUYKENDALL, DENNIS DECKER AND TO BILL MCCONNELL WHO PHOTOGRAPHED MUCH OF THE WORK INCLUDED IN THIS BOOK. • TO MY FAMILY, FOR THEIR CONTINUING SUPPORT. I AM GRATEFUL TO ALL THE DESIGNERS, ARTISTS AND PHOTOGRAPHERS WHO CONTRIBUTED THEIR STUNNING WORK FOR PUBLICATION. • FINALLY, LOUISE HUNNICUTT, FOR HER PATIENCE, SIGNIFICANT CONTRIBUTIONS, UNDERSTANDING AND ENCOURAGEMENT OF THIS EFFORT.

HiP STUFF· CHAOTIC · PROVOCATIVE ·
Existential + Freedom·
dislocated · radical + E
Conflict·Indelicate · Fragmen
Eccentric · MUTANT· s
Different · Immoral ·
urge · IRREGular · WILD · iL
Funky · wacko · BAd
liberal · unortho
Poetic · unschooled · Anti·Soc
Screwed uP · FuTur
revolutionary · inte
DoGMA · buffoonery · Mocke
contemporary · sup
wrinkled·HIDDEN · Resi